Praise for Ba

"*Balance With Grace* is a wonderful gift of encouragement that offers strategies for success to all who want to live more joyfully in the world. I love the practical, heart-centered exercises Grace Durfee presents. She truly helps you access your soul's wisdom to enable you to celebrate life."

—Lynn Robinson, author of *Divine Intuition* and *Trust Your Gut*

"In her book, *Balance with Grace,* Grace Durfee shares her life experiences and wisdom, offering wonderfully practical approaches to everyday living. Gently escorting us through the seasons, she helps us celebrate accomplishments, avoid common pitfalls, honor our past, and most importantly, create our present and future with clarity and intention, all toward an ongoing life of balance and grace."

—Alan Seale, Leadership and Transformation Coach
Author of *Soul Mission, Life Vision* and *Intuitive Living*

"In the modern world, our most valuable commodity is time. *Balance with Grace* provides a wealth of thoughtful exercises and simple strategies for choosing how your precious time will be spent. Grace Durfee's realistic and practical solutions for enjoying a more balanced lifestyle will help you create more joy and satisfaction in your life and work."

—C.J. Hayden, Master Certified Coach, author of *Get Clients Now!* and *Get Hired Now!*

"A wonderful, thoughtful book with great resources and ideas for anyone seeking greater balance."

—Sharon Teitelbaum, Master Certified Coach,
author of *Getting Unstuck Without Coming Unglued: Restoring Work-Life Balance,* www.stcoach.com

"Grace Durfee is truly a new kind of grace in the world. She's a modern day woman who synergistically sources a wonderful family, a fantastic coaching practice, a great leadership role in the US coaching community, and on top of all that, a brilliant new book that will help others to fulfill their lives. If you want grace and fulfillment in all that you do, dive in and take it from Grace!"

—Soleira Green, global visionary,
and author of *The New Visionaries,* www.newvisionaries.net

"Struggle is strictly overrated! In this powerful book, Grace Durfee outlines a sound strategy for not just achieving balance in your life, but creating harmony between all the 'have-to's' and the 'want-to's' of life."

—Kim George, CEO of The AQ Institute, *Coaching Into Greatness: 4 Steps to Success in Business and Life*, www.AQInstitute.com

Motivational, inspiring, authentic and accessible, *Balance with Grace* beautifully explores the seasons of life while providing many avenues for your own self-discovery and conscious creation. It is the perfect gift (of grace) for anyone who is looking for more balance in their life, (maybe you?)

—Deb Busser, speaker, coach, author of *New Easy Women*, www.neweasywomen.com

Balance with Grace not only helps readers who have super busy lives become more aware of their lifestyle choices; it guides them to make more conscious choices so that they can create the life they want to be living. Grace includes an abundance of resources and powerful insightful questions that allow the reader to dig deeper into their soul and spirit when redesigning their life.

—Natalie Gahrmann, work/life effectiveness coach and author of *Succeeding as a Super Busy Parent*

"Grace Durfee has found artful solutions on the central dilemma of our "go for it lives" in her new book *Balance with Grace*. She openly reveals her own challenges and the process of making thoughtful choices, as she leads the reader through the opportunities we all face in our quest for joy. *Balance with Grace* resonates with genuine strategies for multitasking families. I enjoyed the colorful, practical analogies from the author's experiences and the spontaneous spirit of celebration that is infused in the pages of this new and helpful text. Thank you for helping us all keep the joy in our hearts."

—David Sollars M.Ac. Lic. Ac., author of *The Complete Idiot's Guide to Acupuncture and Acupressure* and *The Complete Idiot's Guide to Homeopathy*

"*Balance With Grace* is a fabulous resource book for those who are over-extended and busier than ever, but still looking for relief, meaning, and balance. Read it all at once, refer to it daily or weekly, or use it as a seasonal planning tool for inspiration. It's a wonderful compendium of resources, strategies, and methods to find grace and balance, no matter what your situation."

—Kerul Kassel, author of *Productive Procrastination* and *Stop Procrastinating Now*, www.stopprocrastinatingnow.com

Balance with Grace

Celebrate the Kaleidoscope of Life

by

Grace Durfee

*AuthorHouse™
1663 Liberty Drive, Suite 200
Bloomington, IN 47403
www.authorhouse.com
Phone: 1-800-839-8640*

*First published by AuthorHouse 1/22/2008
ISBN: 978-1-4343-3967-6 (sc)*

Library of Congress Control Number: 2007907626

*Printed in the United States of America
Bloomington, Indiana*

This book is printed on acid-free paper.

Other works by Grace Durfee

Called to Coaching?
Discover if Coaching is the Career for You

Success with Grace:
Grow a Profitable and Fulfilling Coaching Business

To
Bill, Sam, and Alex,
with love.

TABLE OF CONTENTS

Introduction

When my sons were younger and I was in the habit of reading them bedtime stories, I remember reading aloud a book about knights in medieval times. The book described the Dark Ages as a time when people had to work very hard just to put food on the table and keep a roof over their heads. People didn't have much time for leisure, and the arts and culture stagnated. Sounds eerily familiar, doesn't it? How often do you hear or voice complaints about how much there is to do, how there's not enough time, or how difficult life is? Isn't it time to stop struggling and discover how to balance with grace?

Since the early 1990s, there's been an increasing amount of attention given to work/life balance. The media, books, workshops, and entire conferences have explored strategies for attaining balance and enjoying a higher quality of life. There's evidence that this focus has made a positive impact with trends toward:

- people living longer, more productive lives. Retirement has been redefined as "the third age" as seniors now lead active, vibrant lives into their eighties and beyond.

- greater affluence. Instead of aiming for a chicken in every pot, most households now own at least one car and computer.

- increased interest in the mind/body/spirit connection. Yoga and meditation are becoming mainstream, not alternative, practices.

- people placing a higher value on taking care of themselves. Nutritional supplement, skin care, and spa industries have grown exponentially.

Even businesses have jumped on the balance bandwagon. With the increase of working mothers, single-parent families, and employees in the "sandwich generation," companies have responded with more family-friendly programs and policies. Corporations vie for an opportunity to be included in *Working Mother* magazine's annual ranking of the 100 Best Companies—the family-friendliest companies in America. Benefits such as child care, flex-time, tele-commuting, wellness programs, and more liberal family (not only maternity) leave and other paid-leave days contribute to balance and increased productivity. They also help companies attract and retain employees.

That's the good news. On the flip side, with the advent of a competitive global economy and the opportunity to outsource, many companies have cut staff and slashed "balance" programs to meet tighter budgets. This has placed a greater demand upon remaining employees. Many people are working longer and harder than ever. Stress has become epidemic. We multi-task our way through over-scheduled days. We are also training our children to follow this same path as we sign them up for multiple after-school sports and activities. Although there's been some progress, for the vast majority of people there's still a gap between reality and their desired quality of life. If all "dis-ease" stems from a lack of balance, as Eastern medicine teaches, here are some sobering statistics:

- An estimated 66% of American adults are either overweight or obese, with noticeable increases over the last twenty-five years.[1]

- Chronic diseases, such as heart disease, stroke, cancer, chronic respiratory diseases and diabetes, which take a tremendous toll on quality of life, are now responsible for 60 percent of deaths worldwide.[2]

- The number of sleeping pill prescriptions has increased in the US by 60% since 2000, with 42 million prescriptions filled in 2006. The National Institute of Health has found that 10 to 15 percent of the general population suffers from chronic insomnia.[3]

- Traditional family dinners are disappearing in our culture, with more meals being eaten out or in front of the television. A staggering one in four Americans visits a fast food restaurant daily.[4]

Despite many strides forward, the cry for balance seems more urgent than ever.

Yet of course, we have unquestionably made progress since medieval times. We certainly have far more choices. We are masters of our own domain, not serfs toiling under a feudal lord. For the most part, the shape our lives are in is our responsibility, and if we aren't completely satisfied, we can do something about it. We hold the keys to change.

You hold it in your power to enjoy a balanced, fulfilling life. This book is designed to help you become more aware of your lifestyle choices and more committed to creating the life you want. This book will help you learn to make decisions, not by default, but with intention for what supports you and your happiness. Instead of fighting change, which is inevitable, you'll learn to work with it. You'll learn how to celebrate the process as well as the results.

So, what makes me an expert on balance? Since opening my coaching company in 2000, I've helped hundreds of busy professionals, career changers, and small business owners achieve professional success while enjoying more balanced lives. I've supported them in making choices and changes uniquely suited to their life circumstances and goals.

It's just as much, however, from the learning experiences on my personal journey as a balance-seeker that I write. They say that you teach what you most need to know. That's certainly true in my case. It's taken me a while to learn that I'm only effective when I've taken care of myself. As a busy, self-employed, married, mother of two, with many interests and goals, I know all too well the feeling of being pulled in multiple directions. I have firsthand experience with the on-going challenge to do good work, be a loving wife and mother, manage a household, and find time to nurture myself. Rather than complaining about feeling scattered or overwhelmed, I prefer to think of myself as a "Renaissance woman" who thrives on variety. Through the ever-changing phases of life, I do my best to make choices that honor my priorities and promote balance. During my years as a stay-at-home mom, for instance, when I found myself feeling cranky and depleted from meeting everyone else's needs, I sought ways to feed my body, mind and spirit. I joined a baby-sitting co-op to free up time for myself, began playing on a competitive tennis team, resumed piano lessons after a twenty-year break, and participated in women's spirituality groups through my church. As a result, my children and I all grew during this period. In my work, I encourage others to do the same.

It doesn't really matter, however, if I'm a balance expert or not, for you are the expert in your own life. As a coach I've learned that people are most successful when they access and act upon their own inner wisdom instead of being told what to do. Therefore,

I'm not passing on a foolproof recipe for balance that must be precisely followed with no substitutions. I'm not even presenting a fixed menu. Instead, I'm inviting you to a sumptuous banquet where you can select from a myriad of strategies, tools, and techniques to find what's most satisfying. Since we all have different tastes, some approaches will immediately appeal to you, others may not. Do be adventurous, and be willing to sample the unfamiliar. All are served up to help you attain and sustain balance.

How to use this book

Regardless of what time of year you begin reading this book, I recommend that you start with "Beginnings" as it sets the stage for the rest of the book. In "Beginnings" you will make an honest assessment of your life in its present state and be given tools and a framework for making changes that support balance.

You'll derive the greatest benefit from this book if you *experience* as well as read it. You may want to record your discoveries and progress in a separate journal or notebook. Feel free to write in the book as well, as long as it's your copy. You'll notice that there are open bullets beside questions and bits of information. You could shade in the bullets next to the questions and tips that resonate with you. Or you can shade in bullets of the questions you've answered and the information you've applied. Suggested actions and approaches are set off by open arrow bullets. Likewise, you could shade them to keep track of your progress or intended actions.

While you certainly may read the book from cover to cover, the next sections are arranged by season. You may want to jump to the section that corresponds to the current season after completing "Beginnings." Following the calendar year, these sections begin with "Late Winter and New Year" (for those of us in the Northern Hemisphere) and move through "Spring," "Summer," and "Fall," coming full circle to end with "Early Winter and Holidays."

Feel free to skip around and use the index to find topics that most closely correspond to your current concerns. Or open the book at random, trusting that it will open to a message that you need to receive in that moment. You may choose to savor the readings one morsel at a time or opt to read entire sections in one sitting. However you engage with this book, may it serve you well as a guide to greater joy and balance.

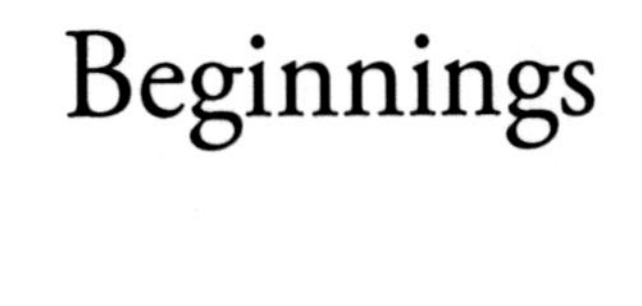
Beginnings

DEFINITIONS

Balance

What are your beliefs about balance? Do you think it's an elusive state that, like the Fountain of Youth, people can spend a lifetime seeking, but never attain? Or do you believe that it's Nature's way and the path we are intended to follow? This exercise will help you better understand your definition of balance.

1. What three different words or short phrases come to mind when you think of balance? Write each in one of the large circles of the Venn Diagram found on the opposite page.

2. Choose two words from your circles, and consider, if both of these are present in your life, what does that create? Write this new word or phrase in the space where the two circles intersect.

3. Continue doing this for the other two overlapping circles.

4. Finally, look at the three new words or phrases you came up with in the intersections. If all of these are true for you, what does this yield? Write the word or phrase best describing this state or feeling in the center, rounded triangle of the Venn Diagram.

BALANCE VENN DIAGRAM

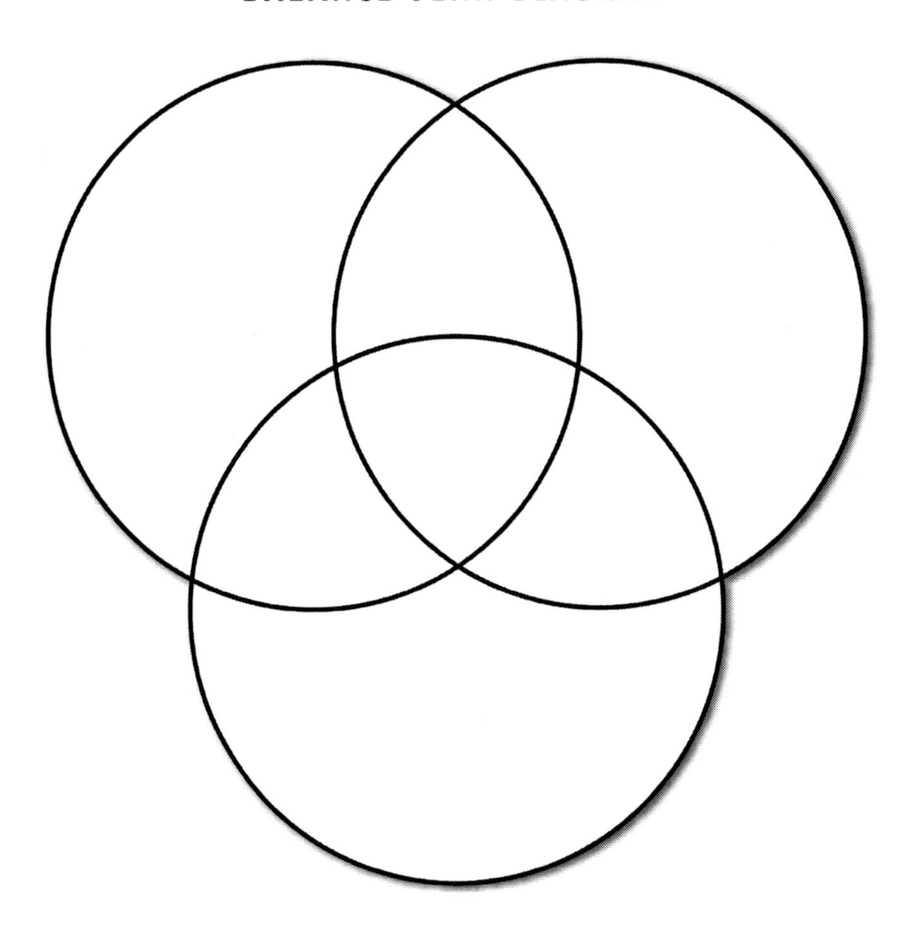

There are twenty-five definitions of balance in my Random House edition of *Webster's College Dictionary*, including:

- a state of equilibrium or equipoise
- mental or emotional steadiness
- equality between the totals of two sides of an account
- the power or ability to decide an outcome
- the harmonious integration in an artistic work
- to arrange or adjust the parts of symmetrically
- to be equal or proportionate to
- to estimate the relative importance of

From my perspective, balance is the feeling that all is well. It's a state of being characterized by feelings of appreciation and acceptance of yourself, of others, of your environment, and of your present circumstances. Balance doesn't mean that everything in your life is perfect, with all to-dos checked off your list and no loose ends. Life isn't like a bed that can be made with the military precision of hospital corners, with everything neatly tucked in. Everything evolves and is ever-changing.

Being in balance means that you are happy with where you are right now and with the direction you are taking. Telltale clues may include contented sighs, smiles, and joyful, vibrant energy. Signs of imbalance may manifest as frowns, complaints, physical discomfort, feelings of being overwhelmed, and stress. These moments may be fleeting or prolonged. The aim of this book is to extend your periods of balance and to provide tools to regain your balance when you feel yourself beginning to wobble.

Grace

Grace is another word that can be hard to define. Here's an exercise that will help you explore your understanding of the word grace. I've adapted it from a cluster writing activity I learned from my current coach, Alan Seale. Gather a number of sheets of paper. Beginning with the first sheet, write down the word "grace" and all the words that come to mind when you think of grace. When you've run out of words, take the last word you came up with and write that on another piece of paper. On that page, list all the words you can think of which relate to that word. Continue the process until you feel like you've reached a stopping point or have reached a moment of insight. Reflect or journal about any revelations you had during this experience.

Once again, *Webster's College Dictionary* offers multiple definitions for grace, including:

- elegance or beauty of form, manner, motion or action
- attractive ease and smoothness of movement
- mercy; clemency; pardon
- the freely given, unmerited favor and love of God
- the influence or spirit of God operating in humans
- a virtue or excellence of divine origin
- a short prayer before or after a meal in which blessings are asked and thanks is given
- to adorn: Many paintings graced the walls.
- to favor or honor: to grace an occasion with one's presence

The meanings of grace that resonate the most with me are: a presence characterized by ease and flow and an unconditional gift from the Divine. I've often felt that when my parents named me Grace they gave me awfully big shoes to fill. Many times I've doubted my capacity to live up to my name.

I have a hunch that we naturally operate from a place of grace as children. We may not actually fall from grace as we get older, but I think, as adults, many of us need to reawaken to the grace in our lives. My mother has often recounted a story from when I was four years old, which reinforces my belief. I've always had platinum blonde hair and as a child was quite a towhead. One day in an ice cream parlor with my family, a waitress asked me where I got such beautiful hair. Without hesitation I matter-of-factly replied, "God gave it to me." It's taken me several decades to sort out my spiritual beliefs and return to the acceptance of a divine order that I experienced as a child. Now I'm aware of grace on a daily basis. I also no longer want to change my name. I'm very happy with Grace.

~~~~~~

Resources:

Everyday Grace: Having Hope, Finding Forgiveness, and Making Miracles, by Marianne Williamson

The Unmistakable Touch of Grace: How to Recognize and Respond to the Spiritual Signposts in Your Life, by Cheryl Richardson

Grace (Eventually): Thoughts on Faith, by Anne Lamott
~~~~~~

Kaleidoscope of Life

As much as we'd like to be able to "freeze frame" or permanently hold moments in balance, life resists our attempts to create unwavering stability. I've been practicing yoga for years and am particularly fond of standing balance poses. What I've discovered in these poses is that I cannot be rigid. In fact, rigidity is a sure route to failure. This means that, even though I'm tempted, I can't lock my knees or hold my breath when I've reached the height of the posture. I also need to accept the inevitable wobbles. Like a tightrope walker, I must constantly make shifts and slight adjustments to stay balanced.

So it is with our lives. Flexibility and agility help us adjust to ever-changing circumstances. Like a kaleidoscope, the many pieces of our lives are always in flux, settling into new patterns, only to shift again. We may long to preserve a design that's particularly pleasing, but eventually some elements will change.

When my sons were infants I was always thrilled when it seemed that they had finally settled into a schedule. Life would go so smoothly when they were in a routine of sleeping and eating at regular times. We'd have a few days when I'd think, "Hey, this is easy!" Then one of them would get sick or start cutting a new tooth, throwing everything off kilter.

Life is like a kaleidoscope, revealing ever-changing patterns. A new design may last for a matter of days, weeks, or months before shifting again. Occasionally elements might stay the same with only subtle variations, but sometimes all new colors, shapes, and elements appear, producing a picture that looks nothing like the old one.

You may at times intentionally twist your kaleidoscope to start over by redesigning your life, perhaps through sweeping job, relationship, or location changes. During a pivotal point in my mid-twenties, I made all of these changes simultaneously. I moved to Boston from Philadelphia, started a new job in a different field, and ended a relationship of five years, less than two months before our planned wedding.

Sometimes the basic design remains the same, but the colors vary, in much the same way that trees in New England change with the seasons. An example of this in our family is the way our sports change with the seasons. I prefer to be a seasonal athlete, walking and gardening in the spring, swimming and playing tennis in the summer, hiking and jogging in the fall, and cross-country skiing and snowshoeing in the winter. My sons mix it up as well. They rotate from football and soccer practice in the fall, to basketball and skiing in the winter, and later to lacrosse and track in the spring. Just when I get into a groove with carpooling and game schedules, the sport seasons are over and a new pattern begins.

Sometimes we move our own kaleidoscope's lens to set the shards tumbling. Sometimes other people knock into us, creating a new pattern. Sometimes an unseen force, grace, perhaps, imposes change upon us. Sometimes the change in seasons shakes things up for us. Regardless of how much control we had over the transition, we always determine how we respond to the emerging design. We can learn to make the most of any situation, recalibrating and rearranging when necessary. What we make of the changing patterns and how we feel about them is what determines our state of balance or imbalance.

Notice that the process I'm offering isn't a one-page, ten-step bulleted list detailing the way to balance. That's because there is no single, secret formula for balance. Just like snowflakes with their kaleidoscope-like designs, each of us is unique. So are our preferences. One individual's ideal balance could be devastating to another.

We all must find our own way to balance. Others may offer valuable guidance, but they cannot provide balance for us. Think about how a child learns to walk. He or she usually takes the first unsteady steps while clinging tightly to the hands of a patient, stooped over grown-up. Eventually, he or she has to let go and learn to balance and walk alone. Like that supportive grown-up, this book offers guidance and encouragement. Like the toddler, you are the one who must take the steps in order to move forward.

Welcome to the journey.

BALANCE EXERCISES

There are a number of tools that can help you assess your life and develop a plan to create greater balance and satisfaction. They will give you a framework for exploration and change.

The first tool is the **Balance Wheel** (also known as the Wheel of Life). This popular coaching tool will give you a holistic, big picture view of your life. It's designed to help you take stock of how satisfied you are with the different facets of your life. It will give you a good sense of your starting point and can be used as a measuring device to note your progress as you work through the book.

The accompanying **Considerations** poses questions to help you reflect upon what's working well for you and what's not in the major areas of your life. You can note the positives and negatives on the **Balance Sheet**.

Finally, the **Stepping Stone exercise** will help you clarify what you want, while the **Stepping Stone form** helps you chart a course for desired changes. The form also allows you to visually track your progress as you bridge the gap between where you are and where you'd like to be.

Balance Wheel

Assessing your life with the Balance Wheel
It's best to undertake this assessment when you feel even-keeled. For instance, if you are in despair over a recent upheaval in your life or are euphoric after receiving exciting news, the results may be skewed. Do the exercise when your emotions settle into what's closer to normal for you.

First, take a look at the segments of the Balance Wheel to see if they accurately represent the major aspects of your life. Feel free to rename, add, or delete areas so they truly depict your life. Here's how I would define the different areas:

Work: your vocation, your productive efforts—both paid and unpaid

Abundance: your financial state, your blessings

Wellness: physical health, stress/relaxation level

Relationships: your connection and involvement with others

Leisure: pastimes, pursuits in your non-working hours

Discovery: personal evolution and learning

Spirit: relationship with a Higher Power, your attitude

Environment: your physical surroundings, where you spend your time

BALANCE WHEEL

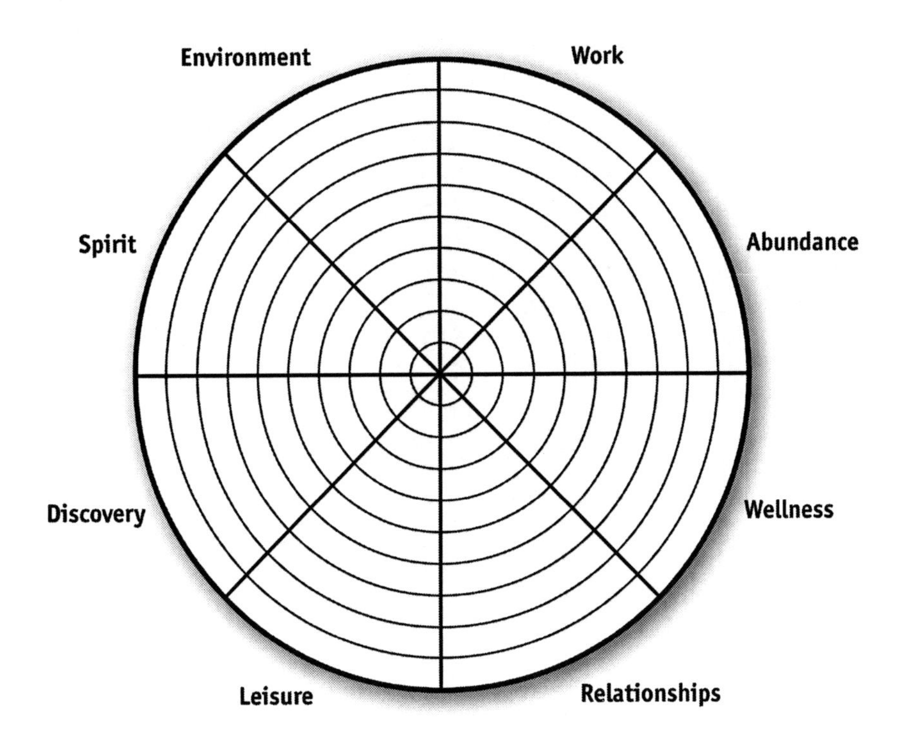

Next, pick any segment of the wheel. As you reflect on this area, pick a number from zero to ten that best represents how happy you currently are with that part of your life. A zero would indicate total dissatisfaction or lack. A ten would mean that you are extraordinarily satisfied and can see no possible need for improvement. Shade out from the center to the line that represents your level of satisfaction. Work your way around the wheel, until you've considered and appropriately shaded each section.

Now, look at the total picture of your completed wheel. Are some shaded areas larger than others? This is quite typical. I've yet to see a wheel with all the spokes shaded out to the outermost "ten" level or even with completely even outer edges. What does the current configuration of your wheel mean for your life? Imagine that you, like my younger son, could easily ride a unicycle. If this wheel was the tire of your unicycle, what kind of ride would you have? The greater your levels of satisfaction, the larger the wheel and the more ground you'd cover with each pedal stroke. A small wheel requires a tremendous amount of effort to cover even the shortest distance.

Applying the Balance Wheel
You can pinpoint the areas that are noticeably lower than others and brainstorm ways to increase your satisfaction.

- What makes you give this aspect of your life a low rating?
- What would be more fulfilling?
- What actions are required to expand your satisfaction in this area?

You can look for ways to sustain your current levels of satisfaction.

- What does it take to maintain your current level of contentment?
- What are your minimum daily/weekly/monthly requirements in each area?
- How can you make sure you do these things?

You can further enhance what's already working. Often actions create ripple effects with successes in one area leading to successes in others.

- What are the real gems, the most pleasing parts of your life?
- What would make you rate these sections with tens?
- What steps can you take to further refine and polish these areas?

You can use the Balance Wheel as a tool for measuring change. It offers you a visual representation of how you feel at a particular moment. It's natural for your levels of satisfaction to expand and contract, like an accordion. Periodically, download a blank form from my website www.balancewithgrace.com and revisit the Balance Wheel to note what's shifted. You may want to do this at the beginning of each season, on your birthday, or when you are feeling particularly reflective. It is helpful to date each balance wheel, and make a journal entry or write a few lines on the back of the form about what is happening in your life. For instance, to give us a snapshot of their starting points, my coaching clients complete a Balance Wheel when we begin working together. Every few months they fill out a new one as they review accomplishments and set new goals. Improvements can be dramatic, such as the jump in the work area after a burnout client leaves a dreaded job to pursue his dream business or in the relationship area when a lonely single meets someone and begins dating seriously.

You can use your collection of completed Balance Wheels as a visual reminder. It can serve as a prompt to keep you mindful of how you are integrating all aspects of your life. It can help you celebrate your on-going journey and anticipate the exciting possibilities that lie ahead.

As revealing as the Balance Wheel is, it's obviously an oversimplification of life. Like kaleidoscopes, our lives have many facets. There are many more than eight spokes in our Balance Wheels. Each section of the wheel could be further subdivided to more accurately represent the people, places, and things to which we give our time and energy.

Here are some additional subsets. You may want to come up with even more:

Work: contribution, colleagues, clients, challenge, creativity, competence
Abundance: life planning, savings, income, spending, charity, debt, insurance protection, legacy, gratitude

Wellness: diet, exercise, stress management, physical health, vitality/energy, sleep
Relationships: significant other/spouse/partner/lover, friends, immediate family, extended family, community, pets
Leisure: vacation, recreation, hobbies, creativity, adventure, humor, fun
Discovery: spiritual, intellectual, emotional, physical, sexual, social, psychological
Spirit: spiritual/religious community involvement, prayer life, meditation practice, peace, flow, attitude
Environment: home, office, yard, vehicle, neighborhood, region/habitat/climate, nature

We don't live our lives in neat little compartments. There's overlap and interplay between all of the many, complex aspects of our lives. For instance, one of my favorite times of the year is the week in July that we spend camping in the mountains. My husband and boys go up a few days before I do to have a few days of "male bonding" with my brother-in-law and nephew. I then get to enjoy a few rare days of having the house to myself. I often spend time doing some of my favorite things: gardening (environment), reading, writing, meditating (discovery and spirit), swimming (wellness). Often I will work part of the time (work) and may schedule get-togethers with one or more friends (relationships). I enjoy keeping the house clean with only myself to pick up after (environment). Then I drive up to the mountains to meet them. I usually listen to a non-fiction audio book (discovery). My sister-in-law and nieces (relationships) join us as well. We share lots of great hikes, meals, (wellness) and campfire songs and stories (leisure).

There's rarely an even distribution of time and energy between these different areas. It would be nearly impossible to always equally portion out our time and energy into each Balance Wheel section. There may be times in our lives when we have a very lopsided-looking wheel, when one or more parts predominate. For instance, tending an infant demands so much attention, that self-care, on a good day for a new parent, means actually managing to shower. But the baby thrives, and eventually the needs of both parent and child are met. Likewise, if we are in the throes of starting a new business, the bulk of our energy and attention will go toward work. A new business launch requires a tremendous investment of time, focus, and money. During the start-up phase, social life, hobbies, and vacations may temporarily be placed on hold. This intentional imbalance can be effective. If attention was evenly dispersed, the business might never get off of the ground.

One client in the personal development business, for example, found he needed to put in long hours and work part of the weekends to develop content and materials for his seminars. As his business took off and he trained others to facilitate the program, he enjoyed making up for lost family time with visits to a nearby Disney theme park.

Trouble arises when temporary imbalances become permanent, for example, when a hardworking business owner becomes a workaholic or a nurturing mother becomes a self-sacrificing martyr who has lost her sense of self.

You can view the Balance Wheel as a pie chart and decide how large a slice you'd like from each section. What are the most pleasing proportions for you right now? Fill out the following blank wheels, one for weekdays, and the other for weekends, to remind yourself of your preferences. Feel free to create your own labels for each section.

There's nothing static about balance or life. The borders and satisfaction levels of your Balance Wheel will fluctuate over time. As you work through this book, my hope is that your Balance Wheel will continue to expand, to reflect an increasingly fulfilling life.

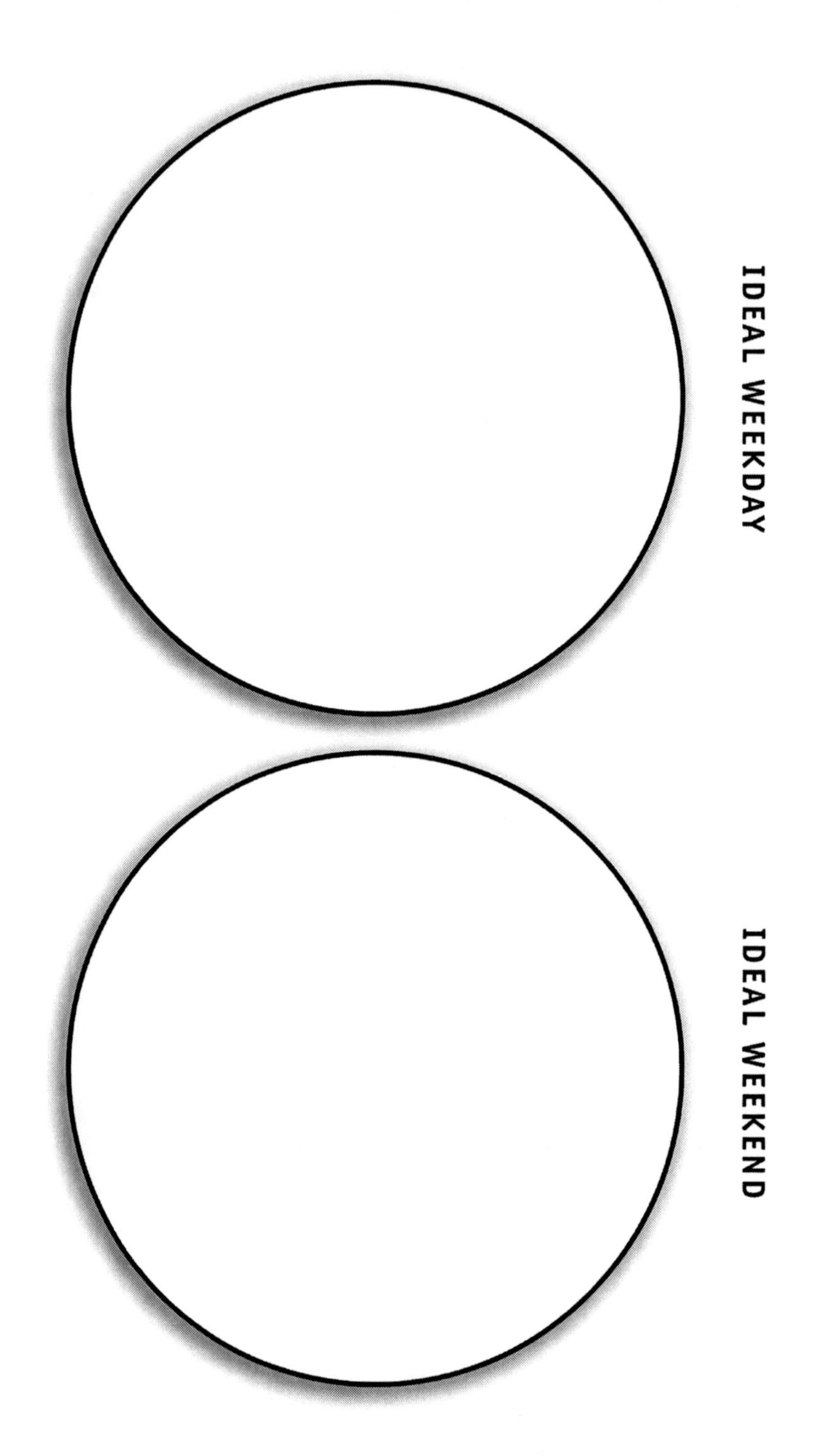
IDEAL WEEKDAY
IDEAL WEEKEND

Considerations

Work

- o How do you contribute?
- o How often do you take work home with you?
- o How fulfilling is your work?
- o What natural gifts and talents are you using in your present work?
- o How do you feel returning to work after a weekend or vacation?
- o How stimulating do you find your work, your colleagues, and your work environment?
- o How well do your work and your company's culture align with your core values?

Abundance

- o How rich do you feel?
- o What are you saving for and how much have you saved toward this goal?
- o What is enough for you?
- o Where are you financially irresponsible?
- o Do you have a scarcity (half-empty) or abundance (half-full) mentality?
- o What percentage of your resources (time, money, energy) do you share?
- o How easily do you manifest what you want?

Wellness

- o What is healthy/unhealthy about your present lifestyle?
- o What are your favorite ways to move your body?
- o How frequently and for how long do you exercise?
- o How often do you get sick?
- o How much sleep do you require and how much do you get?
- o What do you need to eat more of or less of to have a nutritious diet?
- o How are you handling stress in your life?

Relationships

- o How comfortable do you feel asking for what you need in your relationships?
- o What legacy are you leaving for your loved ones?
- o How accepting are you of others?
- o How do you handle disagreements and misunderstandings?
- o Who unconditionally loves and accepts you?
- o Who do you unconditionally love and accept?

- o How do you feel before, during, and after visits with extended family?

Leisure

- o How do you relax?
- o What do you do for fun or to recharge?
- o How much time have you spent doing this in the past week?
- o When was your last vacation?
- o How often do you get away from it all, for a weekend or overnight?
- o What's your favorite part of the day and why?
- o How often do you laugh?

Discovery

- o What insights have you had about yourself lately?
- o What lessons are you learning from your current experiences?
- o How are you stretching yourself?
- o Who are you becoming?
- o What are you a role model for?
- o What are you insatiably curious about?
- o What do you most want to learn?

Spirit

- o How often do you feel "in the flow"?
- o What helps you feel connected to your Higher Power/Spirit?
- o What do you find inspirational?
- o Where have you found a spiritual home or community?
- o How do you bring the sacred into the everyday?
- o How often do you operate out of love versus fear?
- o What are your spiritual practices and how often do you engage in them?

Environment

- o How productive and inspiring is your work space?
- o How easy is it for you to find things you need?
- o How aesthetically pleasing is your environment?
- o What do you love about where you live?
- o If you won a complete home makeover, what would you change?
- o What kind of Feng Shui or energetic feel does your living space have?
- o How comfortable are others in your space?

Balance Sheet

If you have your own business or are familiar with accounting, you may have worked with a balance sheet. This is the financial statement that details your assets and liabilities to determine your equity or net worth. This accounting tool gives you a picture of your financial position at a given point in time.

Here's another type of balance sheet, requiring no accounting skills, which you can use to take stock of your life. Think about and then write down in the appropriate column, what you view as the pluses and minuses for each area of your life. Since most people have no trouble reeling off a list of complaints, go ahead and begin with the negatives. Jot down what you feel is wrong, annoying, or could be improved.

But don't dwell there. Move on to the right-hand, positive side to list what's meeting or exceeding your expectations, what's enjoyable, and what's working well in these same areas. Also on the plus side, take into account any unrealized opportunities or untapped potential.

If you need some prompts, use the **Considerations** questions to help you reflect on what's working and what's not in each of these areas of your life.

As an example, some common complaints from the Abundance area include not having enough:

- time
- money
- vacation
- downtime
- help with chores and administrative tasks
- sex
- energy
- fun
- friends
- supportive relationships
- focus
- confidence
- physical activity

On the positive side, many people note that they have plenty of:

- things to do
- ideas
- food
- hobbies and interests
- skills and strengths
- reading material
- faith
- opportunity to exercise
- health
- goals

BALANCE SHEET

	MINUSES	PLUSES
Environment		
Work		
Abundance		
Wellness		
Relationships		
Leisure		
Discovery		
Spirit		

Stepping Stones

The following Stepping Stone exercise will help you plan ways to move toward a more balanced life. You'll work with a guided visualization for part of this exercise. You may want to record yourself reading the visualization or access the recording on the resource page of my website. That way, you can listen to the recording and follow voice cues instead of having to read and visualize at the same time. You will want to refer to your completed Balance Wheel and have a blank Stepping Stone form with you for this exercise. You can download full-page versions of both forms from the resource page of my website www.balancewithgrace.com.

Visualization

Imagine yourself setting out for a walk in the woods on a warm spring morning. Rays of sunlight filter through the trees, illuminating the path in front of you. A fragrant carpet of pine needles cushions your footsteps. You are surprised as you notice a variety of mushrooms created by the recent spring rain, some in common shades of white and brown, others in vibrant oranges, reds, and yellows. There's a light breeze at your back which keeps you cool and propels you forward. A nearby flock of blue jays chatters, and you laugh at the antics of a pair of squirrels engaged in a game of chase. You hear the ripple of running water, and as you round a bend you discover a mountain stream crossing your path. It's early yet, and you have no desire to turn back. The path beyond the stream is especially inviting. It's bordered with soft, emerald patches of moss, and there are stands of white birch on both sides. You want to cross the stream. You know from previous experience how numbing the water is this time of year, so you dismiss the idea of wading across. You notice that the stream bed is filled with a variety of rocks that could make perfect stepping stones. There are a number of places where it looks like you could safely cross to the other side.

STEPPING STONES

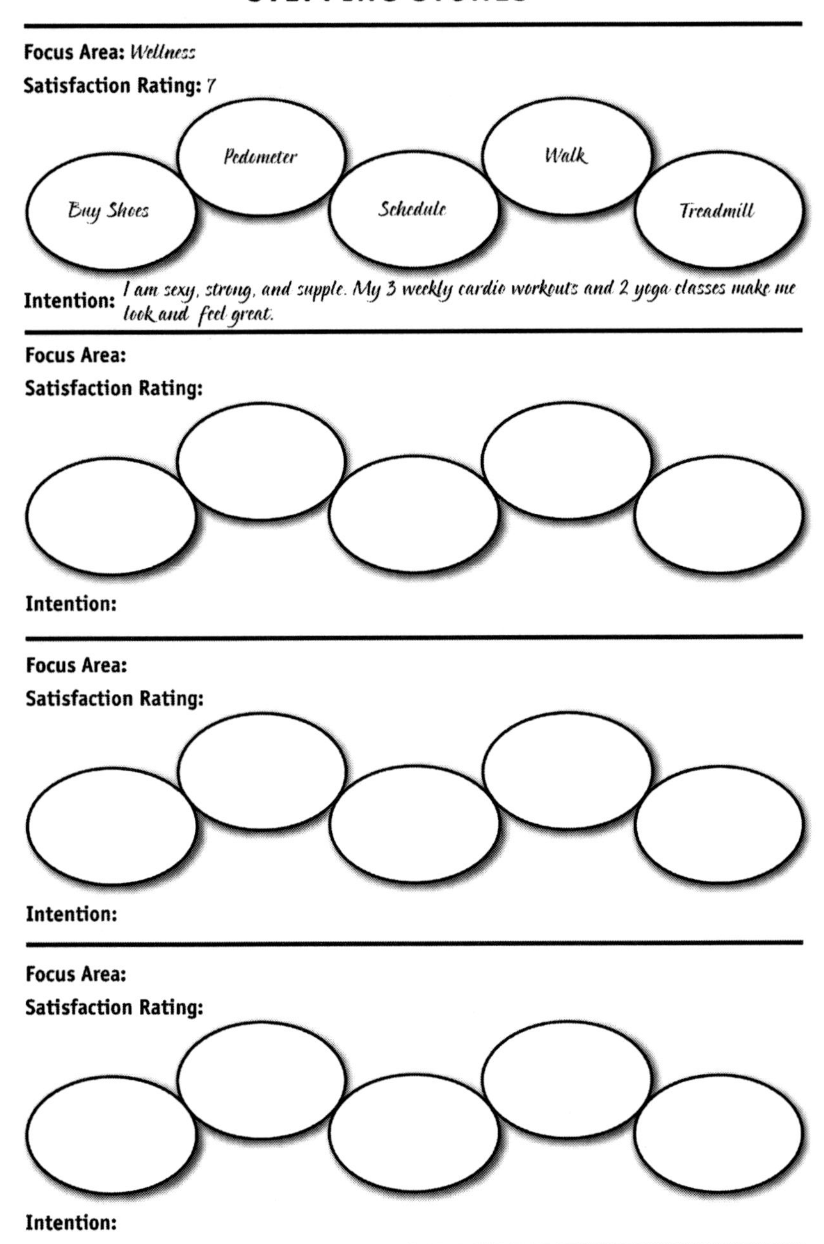

Focus Area: *Wellness*

Satisfaction Rating: *7*

Buy Shoes

Pedometer

Schedule

Walk

Treadmill

Intention: *I am sexy, strong, and supple. My 3 weekly cardio workouts and 2 yoga classes make me look and feel great.*

Focus Area:

Satisfaction Rating:

Intention:

Focus Area:

Satisfaction Rating:

Intention:

Focus Area:

Satisfaction Rating:

Intention:

Incorporating the Stepping Stone form into your visualization, imagine that the left side is your starting point, the spot where you are right now. The opposite bank is where you wish to be, the destination beckoning you forward. The stepping stones are the incremental steps you select to move in the desired direction.

Step one: chose your focus
Beginning on the left bank, select up to three areas from the Balance Wheel (broad categories such as relationships, career, or wellness) as initial priorities. You might select areas that have low Balance Wheel satisfaction ratings or ones that call out to you in some way. Or you might choose an area or two that are already satisfying, that you feel would be easy to enhance and could help you gain momentum for more challenging changes. Pick areas into which you'd be eager to pour some energy and attention. To help you choose, consider:

- What do you *really* want out of life?
- What would give you the most joy?
- What don't you want?
- Continuing on your present path, what regrets will you have ten years from now?
- What's missing?
- What would you like more of in your life?
- What would you like less of?
- Where is your heart pulling you?

In the spaces provided, write down your chosen focus areas as well as the satisfaction ratings you gave them in the Balance Wheel exercise.

For instance:
Focus Area: Wellness
Satisfaction Rating: 6

Step two: set your intention
Select just one focus area to work with at a time. Imagine that you are instantly transported to the opposite side of the bank and that a magical transformation takes place as you step onto it. Suddenly you are doing, being, or having that which you most wished for in this area. It's as if you've landed in the middle of a dream come true. As if you were watching a movie, let the scenes of your vision play out in your mind's eye. Notice all the details and allow your imagination to embellish where you like.

- o What is happening?
- o What does this look and feel like?
- o What's changed?
- o What are you doing differently?
- o What impact does this have?

Now, take a moment to record your intention for this focus area, describing the desired transformation in a phrase or simple sentence. The word "intention" comes from the Latin *intendere,* meaning to stretch toward something. It's fine if your intention feels like wishful thinking or a bit out of reach. The phrasing of your intention is important. Describe the specific outcome you desire as well as the feelings that it will bring. Use present-tense language as if you've already fulfilled your aspiration.

Be positive when you think, speak, and write about your intention because what you focus on is what will expand. Many people struggle, for example, with resolutions to "lose ten (or some other number of) pounds." When articulated in this way, the focus is on the pounds, so that's what sticks around or even grows. An example of a more positively phrased wellness intention is, "I am sexy, strong, and supple. I feel and look great in a size eight (or whatever your ideal size is)."

On the opposite bank, the right-hand side of the form, record your intention for this focus area. Stay with this particular intention as you complete the next three steps. Afterwards, you'll have a chance to repeat the process for the remaining focus areas.

Step three: confirm your desired destination

There are several routes you could take to cross the stream. One would put you slightly above the path, another, below. The straightest course ends in a muddy patch, but you might be able to jump over it. Before immediately plunging forward, it's worth taking the time to determine that you're aiming for a good landing spot. With your intention in mind, consider:

- o Why is this important?
- o Who wants and will benefit from this?
- o How much control do I have here?
- o Is this outcome within the realm of possibility?
- o How will I know when I've reached this goal?
- o How will it feel to have it?
- o Who do I need to become to make this a reality?

Modify or eliminate any intentions that feel like something you *should* want, rather than what you truly do want. Don't adopt someone else's goal unless it mirrors your heartfelt desires. There's nothing joyful or motivating about a "should." With the wellness example, for instance, aim for the size, weight, and level of fitness that feel healthy and ideal for you. Don't allow your goal to be dictated by fashion or fitness magazines.

Step four: plan your next steps

In crossing the stream you want to carefully select the best stepping stones. Look for large ones with flat surfaces. Pick ones that don't look slippery, wobbly, or like too much of a stretch (unless that feels like a fun challenge). Often there's a particular order or logical sequence to the steps, but it's wise to select alternative stepping stones as well. Sometimes a stone looks like a good choice, but as you step on it you realize it won't support you. If you've already identified a substitute, you can quickly switch to that, barely breaking your stride.

In viewing your "dream movie" you may have already seen yourself taking certain actions that led to success. If so, in each oval "stepping stone" of the form, write down the actions you've identified. If you still aren't sure how you could reach your target, use these questions to help you select next steps:

- What needs immediate attention?
- What action(s) would make the biggest difference?
- What are you willing to stop or start?
- What is your next evolutionary step?
- What opportunities are available to you?
- What resources and support do you need?
- What strategies will you employ to meet your goals?
- What are you waiting for?

With the wellness example, for instance, possible stepping stones could include to:

- replace worn out walking shoes
- buy a pedometer to literally measure your progress
- find a walking partner, one who's equally committed to exercise, whose company you enjoy, and who you won't want to let down
- schedule three walking dates a week in your calendar
- walk, setting a specific goal, for example to take 10,000 steps a day

If the final "walk" stone turns out to be a slippery one, for instance if the roads are too snowy and icy to walk safely, you could chose a backup stone. Alternatives might include using a treadmill at the gym or working out at home with an exercise video, DVD, or TV show.

Step five: take each step with full awareness and acceptance

A mindful crossing will lead to success. A mindful crossing means that, while your sights may be set on the opposite bank, as you cross you must be completely conscious of the present and of the stepping stone underfoot at the moment. The stone you step onto may not be where you want to stay; nonetheless, you'll need to make a firm connection with it, at least momentarily. Otherwise you'll slip. Accept that this is where you are for now, and settle into the present moment. Yes, you want to reach the other side, but there's the opportunity to find balance with each new step. The experience of the crossing is just as important as reaching the destination. When you honor the process, you free yourself from the striving trap: always working towards something and living for tomorrow instead of savoring the present.

You'll notice that there are three blank series of stepping stones on the form. This gives you space to develop your intentions and action plans for up to three focus areas. To work on any more than that could make you feel scattered and overwhelmed. Many people work best when they have multiple projects to move back and forth between, giving them flexibility to follow their interest and enthusiasm. If, however, you operate best with a single focus, leave the remaining stepping stones series blank and work only on your top priority.

Other ways to work with Stepping Stones

For some focus areas, five stepping stones may not be enough. You are welcome to add additional stones as you chart your course. Especially if you enjoy brainstorming or thorough planning, use this as an opportunity to capture all of your ideas. Don't, however, look at a long string of stepping stones while you're crossing. This can make you feel dizzy and may make you lose your footing. It's better to use your plans as a map, checking periodically to get your bearings and measure your progress.

On the other hand, if you are having trouble identifying more than one or two steps, don't worry. Remember the wise words of Dr. Martin Luther King, Jr., "Faith is taking the first step even when you don't see the whole staircase." Often after you take the first step or two, the others will be revealed to you.

Our perspective can change once we leave the bank and begin the crossing. What we thought would be a difficult journey could turn out to be surprisingly easy. Or a distance we anticipated covering with a short stride could, on closer examination, require a running start and a leap. As helpful as a plan can be, don't be afraid to abandon it mid-stream if it no longer serves you. A better way may open up for you.

You may also use the five stepping stones to identify the major parts of a long-term project, which may be further broken down into smaller segments. For example, one of my clients used this tool to map out a goal of starting a new business. Some of her stepping stones included: Research, Financing, Systems, Marketing, and Service. Each one of these involved many smaller steps. To stay on track with projects which require multiple phases and many actions, you could create a separate folder for each stepping stone and keep a master list of the sub-steps you've identified.

Place the form where you can see it frequently: on the refrigerator, an office wall, or beside the bathroom mirror. To help you visually chart your progress, color in each stone as you complete the action(s) that you have assigned to it.

FIRST STEPS

Picture This

Setting goals, determining measurable milestones, and consistently taking action are certainly good ways to move forward toward what you want in life. There's another fun activity I often use with clients and workshop participants that can jump-start the process. It's a collage-making activity, and the end product is called a dream map, treasure map, or dream board. Dream maps are powerful tools for self-discovery and manifestation. They are based on a timeless concept: that clearly picturing and creating a visual image of a desired outcome helps it come true. If drawing cave paintings helped ancient people prepare for a successful hunt, imagine what a pictorial wish list could do for you. So, set aside half an hour, bring your passions, aspirations, and intentions, mix them with paper, scissors, glue sticks, and magazines, and see what takes shape!

To prepare for this activity, collect a stack of ten to fifteen magazines and catalogs that you won't mind dismantling. You'll need some type of adhesive: a glue stick, rubber cement, or tape, and a pair of scissors. For the background, use a poster board, oversized construction paper, newspaper, or a large piece of drawing paper. If you have a choice of colors, select your favorite for the background.

Before you begin, spend a few minutes setting your intention for the exercise. Think about what you'd like to manifest in your life.

- What would you like more of?
- What's missing from your life right now?
- What may already be in your life that you'd like to devote more time to?
- What gaps became apparent as you completed the Beginnings exercises?

Now, quickly leaf through the magazines and tear or cut out pages with images that appeal to you. Don't analyze or question why you're selecting certain pictures; if something catches your interest, makes you smile, or say "Yes!" then it's a keeper. You may find you choose images that remind you of a significant place, person, or object from your past or present. Your pictures could represent what you want for the future. Give yourself about twenty minutes to go through the magazines. Then, take your stack of pictures, play with the placement of them, and glue or tape them on the paper when you're satisfied with the arrangement. Feel free to add your own drawings to complete your dream map.

Some people choose to hang their finished dream maps where they'll see them several times a day. Popular spots include the refrigerator door or an office wall. Others prefer to tuck them away to keep them private. I've used both approaches before with tremendous success. I usually need to create a new dream map every six months because everything comes true. For instance, I once chose pictures of a woman receiving a massage, a Zen fountain, a lone cross-country skier, a smiling gardener pushing a wheelbarrow of harvested vegetables, and a woman doing yoga in her living room. These manifested in my life as:

- a barter arrangement with a massage therapist
- a great deal on a Zen fountain at a discount retailer
- an opportunity to rent a Vermont ski condo located a few miles from a lovely Nordic touring center
- an offer to work an exceptionally fertile garden plot at a nearby horse farm in exchange for tilling the soil and sharing some of the crops
- an exchange of coaching for personalized yoga instruction to help me develop a home practice for when I can't make it to yoga class

Exactly why this happens is somewhat of a mystery, although I have some theories. When you clarify what it is that you want, you are better able to focus your energy and actions to move you in that direction. When you commit your ideas and dreams to paper, whether in words or pictures, you make them more concrete. This helps harness the power of visualization. When you put a desire or an intention out to the Universe, amazing synchronicities and coincidences begin to occur. When you know what you are looking for, you become more aware of opportunities around you that could create the opening you need.

Once you realize how powerful dream maps are, you may want to create separate maps for different areas of your life. You might create maps for each section of the Balance Wheel. Choose a background color that you associate with each area, for instance:

green for abundance, red for relationships, and blue for leisure. Select only images related to that aspect of your life. You could assemble all of your dream maps into a dream book.

Choose a favorite photo of yourself to add to your dream map to claim this as your dream.

Use dream maps as a tool for self-discovery. Select every picture that resonates with you for some reason. I often use dream maps with people who are changing careers to help them explore their interests. If you are trying to reconnect with your passions, this exercise can provide valuable clues.

Other good times to make dream maps include: your birthday or the New Year when you're setting goals for the year ahead, when you're looking for a life partner, when you're starting a family, when you're planning a dream vacation, when you're relocating, when you're building a dream house, when you're looking for a new creative outlet, or when you're planning your retirement.

Have fun creating your dream map! This is one of those activities in which you benefit as much from the process as from the final product.

Write On

At the end of an eight-week teleclass I taught at Coach U, I asked students to share how they'd grown and changed from our work. A number of students mentioned the impact that journaling, one of their homework assignments, had on them. A few people who used to journal but had gotten out of the habit, eagerly picked it back up. Others had never kept any sort of diary and discovered it was a helpful tool to record insights and aspirations, brainstorm, process emotions, organize thoughts, and reflect on their lives. If journaling is a habit you'd like to develop or return to, here are some suggestions to help you get started and get the most from the experience.

How to get started

Buy a journal that speaks to you. Many books stores, department stores, boutiques, and websites carry a wide array. You may have a strong preference for the size, weight, look, and feel of the journal. If this is your very first journal, go with something that's really beautiful that you will want to use frequently. If, like me, you quickly fill journals, you may want to buy in volume and opt for inexpensive journals such as lined composition books.

Use a comfortable pen that has some cushioning, so you won't develop calluses. You want to encourage the words to flow and any discomfort will get in the way.

Designate a particular writing spot. You may have a favorite chair by a window, or you may prefer propping yourself up with pillows to write in bed.

Best practices

Figure out the best time of day for you to write, and do it regularly. Writing daily is ideal so that you can record all that's going on in your life. Some common writing times are first thing in the morning or before bedtime. Julia Cameron, the author of *The Artist's Way* recommends the practice of writing what she calls "morning pages." These are a minimum of three longhand pages that you write early in the morning, ideally as soon as you wake up. Morning pages are a good way to clear the cobwebs, develop a plan for your day, capture your bright ideas, and get creative juices flowing.

Don't edit or censor your writing. Give yourself free reign to write about whatever comes to mind. Don't worry about grammar, punctuation, or spelling. It can help to make your journals for your eyes only.

Harvest your old journals. Birthdays and New Year's Day are great times to reread old journals. Revisiting previous entries helps you celebrate your past and reconnect with abandoned ideas and inspirations whose time may have come.

Don't limit your journal writing to making to-do lists and recording recent happenings. Although it's often easiest to begin with a "mind dump" of what's unfolding in your day-to-day life, don't stop there. Include what's happening in your inner as well as outer life. Journal topics, or even entire journals, may include your blessings, feelings, daydreams and nocturnal dreams, inspiration, flashes of intuition, and successes.

~~~~~~

Resources:

The Artist's Way: *A Spiritual Path to Higher Creativity,* by Julia Cameron

Sark's Journal and Play!Book: A Place to Dream While Awake, by Sark

Writing and Being: Embracing Your Life Through Creative Journaling, by G. Lynn Nelson

Life's Companion: Journal Writing as a Spiritual Practice, by Christina Baldwin

Harvesting Your Journals: Writing Tools to Enhance Your Growth and Creativity, by Rosalie Deer Heart and Alison Strickland
~~~~~~

Stay Positive

Are you naturally optimistic or pessimistic? Are you your biggest cheerleader or your own worst enemy? When asked to do something for the first time, do you start making excuses for all the things that might go wrong, or are you excited by the challenge? As Henry Ford said, "Whether you believe you can do a thing or not, you are right." Set yourself up for success by adopting a "can do" attitude. If you often question your abilities, put yourself down, complain, or make disparaging comments, here are some ways to shift into a positive gear:

Focus on what's working well instead of what isn't
A success log is essentially a brag book about you, a tool you can use to remind yourself of your capabilities. To create a comprehensive success log, begin with the recent past and work your way back to childhood, making a list of all of your accomplishments and wins. Include important milestones such as starting a business, having children, and earning a degree, but don't overlook the smaller victories. For example, in my log I included the time in fourth grade when I pushed past the shaky-finger syndrome to play *Born Free* on the piano for my entire school during an assembly. Update your success log frequently to celebrate and acknowledge your triumphs. You may also create a success log that doesn't include the past but is a record of your successes from this point forward.

Eliminate the word "try" from your vocabulary
Although "try" implies willingness, it contains a measure of self-doubt. It's a wimpy word. Replace "I'll try," with more empowering phrases such as "I will," "I can," "I am," or "I'll do my best." If "try" occasionally slips out of your mouth, remember: "The difference between try and triumph is just a little umph!"—Marvin Phillips

View life as an experiment
When something doesn't work out as well as you'd hoped, call it a trial, not a failure. Mistakes and mishaps can be our greatest teachers if we are open to their lessons. As Thomas Edison said, "Surprises and reverses should be an incentive to great accomplishment. Results? Why, man, I have gotten lots of results! If I find 10,000 ways something won't work, I haven't failed. I am not discouraged, because every wrong attempt discarded is just one more step forward." This attitude served Edison well, as evidenced by his invention of the stock ticker, phonograph, incandescent light bulb, and over a thousand other patented innovations.[5]

Surround yourself with supporters
When you are working towards a goal, launching a new venture, or are in the middle of an important project, persistence is crucial. You don't need critics tearing apart your work, blowing holes in your vision, and shaking your confidence. Let people know that you appreciate their support, and request that they share only constructive feedback.

Change your thoughts if they are limiting your success
You can break out of negative thought patterns. Here's a technique I've successfully used with a number of clients. Find a clear jar to place on your desk, kitchen counter, or someplace where you'll see it frequently. Collect some small objects that can easily fit through the mouth of the jar, and store them near your jar. I recommend rocks for this exercise because, like negative thoughts, they can hurt or cause damage. Over the next few days, put a rock in your jar for each of your negative thoughts. Change each negative thought into a positive one. "I don't know how to do that," can become "I will learn how to do that," or "I know who can help me with this." Empty the rocks every morning to give yourself a fresh start for the day. Watch your total of rocks decrease each day. Imagine the possibilities if you only allowed your mind to be fertile ground for positive thoughts.

Reinforce positive thoughts, words, and deeds
As in the previous exercise, use a clear jar to help you visually track your positive responses. Buy two packets of nasturtium seeds to use as your counters. Seeds, like positive thoughts, hold the possibility of growth. I recommend nasturtium seeds because they are large, easy to grow, and produce edible flowers. They are also particularly resilient, thriving even in poor soil. For each positive, upbeat thought, word, or deed, put a seed in your jar. Continue until your seed packets are empty. Then plant your seeds in your garden or in a pot. Let the emerging plants and the bright blossoms remind you of all that is possible with a positive outlook.

Tune In

We live in a world in which we are constantly bombarded with sounds and messages. We may long to escape from the whine of a neighbor's leaf blower, annoying SPAM, and the interruption of television commercials. Regularly setting aside time to spend in quiet is a simple exercise that can have a profound impact. I have personally found a daily commitment of fifteen to twenty minutes sitting in stillness to be a life-altering experience. There is so much that can come from tuning in and giving yourself the gift of silence: answers to questions, clues for what direction to take, solutions to problems, and inspiration. What you hear may be your intuition, your wise self, answered prayers, a still small voice, God, or Spirit. Regardless of how you define it, it's a valuable source of guidance.

How do you tune in? Have you ever noticed that you often get flashes of inspiration while taking a shower, driving, or taking a walk? The regular practice of quiet encourages these whispers of insight. If this has never been a habit of yours, you may want to begin with five minutes, which will seem like an eternity at first, and gradually lengthen the time. There's no right or wrong way to do this. You don't need to assume a pretzel-like lotus pose to make this work. You could sit in your favorite chair with your eyes closed, lie quietly in a hammock or the grass while watching the clouds, or gaze at a candle while relaxing in the tub.

If you would like guidance about a challenge or dilemma, form a specific question in your mind and then let it go as you relax and enter into stillness. Or come into the quiet with the sole intention of becoming empty, being open to receiving images and insights that may come to you. Without forcing an outcome, become aware of any images, sounds, feelings, or senses of knowing that arise. Intuition, inspiration, Divine guidance, or whatever you may choose to call it, appears in many ways. What comes to you may be in the form of one or more of the following "clairs":

- clairvoyance or "clear seeing": images or visual pictures that can be either moving or still
- clairaudience or "clear hearing": sounds, voices, or snatches of songs
- clairsentience or "clear sensing": body sensations, such as gut feelings or goose bumps
- claircognizance or "clear knowing": knowing or being certain without knowing why

Here's an intuitive exercise that I have adapted from Lynn Robinson's *Divine Intuition.* Use it the next time you are faced with a big decision. Imagine that you are walking in a lush garden. There is a white picket fence that borders another section of the garden. The fence has a number of gates in it: one for each of the options you are considering. In your mind's eye, lift the latch and enter the first gate, which represents your first option. Visualize what lies ahead of and around you. Take a moment to reflect on how your body feels. What do you hear or sense as you are here? Spend as much time as you like observing, sensing, and gathering information. Then, turn around and see yourself retracing your steps, out through the gate, back into the garden. Repeat the process with the next gate(s), which represent your other option(s). Compare the experiences.

I recently used this exercise with a client who was wrestling with a major decision, rather than using a more logical, left-brain approach of weighing pros and cons. She had been feeling overwhelmed and confused as she weighed several different options for her next career move. Within ten minutes of working with this exercise, she was very clear about the choice she wanted to make!

We all have a built-in intuitive ability or a sixth sense. Just like a muscle, the more you use and develop your intuition, the better it will work for you. Whether you consider yourself a skeptic or a psychic, tuning in regularly will help guide you toward fulfilling choices.

~~~~~~

Resources:

The Psychic Pathway: A Workbook for Reawakening the Voice of Your Soul, by Sonia Choquette

Divine Intuition: *Your Guide to Creating a Life You Love* and *Compass of the Soul: 52 Ways Intuition Can Guide You to the Life of Your Dreams,* by Lynn Robinson

Intuitive Living: A Sacred Path, by Alan Seale

Practical Intuition, by Laura Day
~~~~~~

Take Care

I've always been fond of the salutation "Take care," which people commonly use instead of "Goodbye." This parting phrase feels like a blessing, a way of wishing someone well. But it also reminds us that we must play an active role in creating our own wellness.

Many people spend a lot of time taking care of others but don't do much to take care of themselves. Perhaps this is because the Golden Rule, "Do unto others as you would have them do unto you," has been instilled in most of us since childhood. I propose broadening the Rule to include, "Do unto yourself as you do unto others." I encourage people to find ways to care for themselves as well as they care for others. Does that make you squirm? Perhaps your inner critic is whispering, "You can't do that. That's selfish!" In my coaching, I've discovered that such a response is a common stumbling block that many people, especially women, encounter when it comes to caring for themselves. Ultimately, it is a self-defeating view. If we want to have the capacity to give to others, we must learn to nurture ourselves.

If you still have some doubts, recall for a moment the instructions flight attendants give before take-off. They say, "If you are traveling with a small child and there's a loss of cabin pressure, put on your own oxygen mask first before helping your child." I once spoke with a woman who had been in this very situation. When the oxygen masks descended, she panicked. Forgetting the flight attendant's warning, she began to help her son. Suddenly she started to feel woozy. Her quick-thinking ten-year-old son finished putting on his mask, helped her with hers, and said, "Get a grip, Mom!"

When you take very good care of yourself you'll find that you establish a reserve of energy and patience, which allows you to be more generous and loving with those around you. You'll find that your cup "runneth over." Here are some suggestions for filling that cup.

Carve out time for yourself

Love begins at the center, with the self. It then extends and expands outward to family, friends, and the world. To nurture that core of love in the center, you must take time for yourself. One of my former clients shared a clever system for sticking to her commitments to herself. In her calendar, she writes, in ink, regular appointments with "Virginia." These are her dates with herself, although her name isn't Virginia. If someone asks her to schedule an activity that conflicts with these appointments, she replies that she already has a commitment with "Virginia."

Pursue your passion
Once you've freed up some time for yourself, now what? Grab pen and paper, and start making a list of the things you love to do or have always wanted to try. What activities, hobbies, or sports have you've given up that you'd love to resume? My list of passions includes healthy gourmet cooking, playing the piano, reading, and gardening. What's on your list?

Treat yourself
What have you been craving? Have you been dreaming of a full body massage, Godiva chocolates, or a professional pedicure? Don't wait for someone to do something for you. Create your own opportunities. Treat yourself to fresh flowers, a facial, or a weekly sauna. Add some things to your list that make you feel truly pampered.

Relax
Relaxation is an important aspect of self-nurture. There are a multitude of techniques you can use to release tension and find tranquility. These include meditation, breath work or *pranayama*, visualization, and guided relaxation. I use many of these but find that mindfulness meditation is the most accessible. Mindfulness can be practiced anywhere and anytime. Simply allow yourself to be fully present in the moment, and become acutely aware of all of your senses. Try this while eating a strawberry, petting a cat or dog, playing with a child, or making love. Include your favorite ways to relax on your list.

Involve others in your nurturing
Self-nurture doesn't require solitude. Relationships help revitalize us. What activities do you enjoy with your spouse or partner, your kids, friends, or relatives? Add these to your list. My list includes family board games, phone calls with friends, hot tubs and occasional overnight getaways with my husband, potluck dinners with friends, and afternoon tea whenever I'm with my mother. Involving others, especially family members, in your self-care will help keep it a priority.

Create nurturing routines and rituals
The most balanced people I know bookend their days with

nurturing routines and rituals in the morning and at night. Many people start their day with a "power hour." They set aside this time to journal, pray or meditate, read something inspirational, stretch, and eat a healthy breakfast. What would get your day off to a good start?

If you have young children, you've probably witnessed the soothing effects of a bedtime routine. You may encourage relaxation and sweet dreams with a warm bath, story, prayer, cuddle, a soft toy or blanket, and a kiss goodnight. What sort of routine would help you unwind at the end of the day?

Make nurturing a habit

Review the list you've made of activities and interests you would like to pursue, and ask yourself:

- What activities would you like to do regularly to renew your body, mind, and spirit?
- What keeps you at your best?
- What's the ideal timing and frequency of your nurturing habits?

Use the **Nurturing Habits** chart to plan and track your self-care progress. The chart is divided into AM, PM, and anytime habits. "Anytime" activities include actions that you don't do at set times or that you don't do every day. For me, cardiovascular exercise falls into this category. I work out at different times, depending upon the weather, the gym class offerings, and my variable work schedule. I think rest days are important, so some days I don't work up a sweat at all.

You can download the **Nurturing Habits** chart from the resources page of my website www.balancewithgrace.com. You don't need to fill in each blank line with a habit. Go with the actions and the number of activities that you feel will best nurture you. Once you've recorded the habits you want to create, track your progress over the course of the next month. Give yourself a check mark for every day that you do that activity. Repetition is what creates new connections or neural pathways in the brain. According to conventional wisdom, it takes about twenty-one days to make or break a habit. The **Nurturing Habits** form has boxes for each day of the month, giving you plenty of opportunities to develop your new nurturing habits. You don't have to wait for the beginning of the next month to begin. Start today!

Enjoy making self-nurture second nature. It's one of the best things you can do for yourself and your loved ones.

~~~~~~

Resources:

The Comfort Queen's Guide to Life, and *Woman's Comfort Book: A Self-Nurturing Guide for Restoring Balance in Your Life,* by Jennifer Louden

Self-Nurture: Learning to Care for Yourself As Effectively As You Care for Everyone Else, by Alice D. Domar and Henry Dreher

How to Meditate: A Guide to Self-Discovery, by Lawrence LeShan

Meditation for Beginners, by Jack Kornfield (includes a CD with guided meditation instruction)
~~~~~~

Nurturing Habits for the Month of ______________________

		1	2	3	4	5	6	7	8	9	10	11	12	13	14	15	16	17	18	19	20	21	22	23	24	25	26	27	28	29	30	31
AM Habits																																
PM Habits																																
Anytime Habits																																

Late Winter and New Year

Joyful Resolutions Naturally Happen

Happy New Year! Are you having a great start to the New Year? Did you make New Year's Resolutions this year?

There's a wide range of responses to resolutions. Some people relish the fresh start that a new year provides and have boundless ideas and lists of what they'd like to do or change. Others are content with the status quo and prefer not to rock the boat. Many, frustrated by a track record of unmet resolutions, feel jaded and scoff at the process. What's your take on resolutions?

Whether it's exercising, eating healthy foods, or cutting back on caffeine, why is it that people so quickly become disillusioned with their New Year's Resolutions? Would we all be better off simply not making resolutions at all?

I don't think so. I believe we are wise to pay attention to our intentions. There's often a lull after the holidays that invites us to slow down, pause, reflect on the past year, and dream of the year to come. We vow to make changes or at least entertain optimistic fantasies when there are things we want to improve in our lives. Just as an oyster needs an irritating grain of sand before it can produce a pearl, our dissatisfaction provides incentive for change. A new year gives us a chance for a fresh, new beginning and an opportunity for transformation.

But how do we go about creating change that will stick, come February, March, and even May? Most resolutions fail because they seem like a lot of hard work. It's hard to be enthusiastic about something that's a struggle. Take a different approach this year. Make resolutions that are fun, exciting, and make you happy. Go for an enticing outcome, but make sure the process of getting there is enjoyable. My theory is: joyful resolutions naturally happen.

We each have a built-in tool that can help us envision and successfully commit to joyful resolutions. It's an internal compass that I call a Joy-o-meter™. It can tell you if you are heading in the right direction, if you are in danger of veering off course, or if you are completely derailed. Your Joy-o-meter™ can guide you in making decisions about starting, stopping, or changing a particular course of action. Because we are hardwired for happiness, our Joy-o-meter™ always gives a true reading without ever needing to be recalibrated. To consult your Joy-o-meter™, get quiet and relaxed, and then check in with yourself to measure your level of joy. Ask your Joy-o-meter™:

- On a scale from 1-10, how happy am I?
- How joyful would (fill in the blank with whatever is in question)_______________ make me?
- How happy would I be to stop ___________?
- How happy would I be to start ___________?
- What could bring me more joy?
- How happy would I be if I made this change?

In *The Art of Happiness*, the Dalai Lama teaches that being happy is not difficult. It's a matter of discovering what makes you happy and then cultivating that in your life. The Joy-o-meter™ can help you do just that. Have fun using this tool to create and stick to resolutions that magnify the joy in your life.

Shake it Up

At times it feels as if I'm in the middle of a snow globe—one of those decorative objects that, when shaken, makes snowflakes swirl around before slowly settling down again. Sometimes that's exactly what I see when I gaze out the window on a wintry day. In our house it can get just as stirred up inside as outside. In the past few years we've made a lot of changes within our home. Instead of playing a game of musical chairs, we've been playing musical rooms. When my husband first moved his office from New Hampshire into our home, he took over the room that doubled as my office and the guest room. My younger son moved into that room, as well, to have a bigger room than his previous bedroom. I moved my office into his old bedroom. That worked well for a while until we decided that our son needed his own room. Then my husband installed French doors to our living room and moved his office into the sunny back corner of that room. During each of these transitions, we've moved furniture, phone lines, office supplies, books, clothes, and toys.

We are far from done. Like a snowball gathering speed, a makeover in one section of the house has inspired us to spruce up the rest. A dear, interior designer friend and her family, visiting relatives in our area for the holidays, recently came to our home for the first time. We had such fun giving her the house tour. We were delighted that she offered to share her ideas. I wrote down all of her wonderful recommendations for adding more color and details. Since then, we've applied many of her suggestions: rearranging furniture, adding bead boarding under some chair rails, updating window treatments, painting my office, and moving a dresser out of storage. How helpful it is to have an outside, expert opinion!

It feels great to change things around. It's given me a wonderful opportunity to reconfigure my office to create an environment that truly supports me. I now have all files and books within easy reach, have a more ergonomic set-up, and have begun reorganizing my filing system. What a wonderful fresh start for the New Year!

I think it's healthy to periodically shake things up or at least take time to assess the status quo. This applies to all areas of life, not just physical surroundings. A new year is the perfect time for a makeover or a new approach. Here are some questions that may motivate you to do your own rearranging:

- What needs buffing up in your surroundings, your systems, or your way of life?
- What's outdated or stale?
- How can you revamp or breathe new life into it?
- What minor adjustment could make a difference?
- What radical change are you now willing to make?
- How can you design perfect environments at work and at home?
- What aren't you using to its fullest potential?

This year, instead of making resolutions, shake things up, and make a few rearrangements.

~~~~~~

Resources:

Use What You Have Decorating: Transform Your Home in One Hour With Ten Simple Design Principles—Using the Space You Have, the Things You Like, the Budget You Choose, by Lauri Ward
~~~~~~

Stay in Motion, Even in Mid Winter

It's predictable. Every year at mid-winter it begins to happen. The parking lot at the health club, which has been jam-packed for most of the month of January, begins to thin out as February approaches. Motivation and interest in fitness decline in February as post-holiday bills, short daylight hours, and the realization that getting in shape is a long, slow process all conspire to discourage gym-goers. Even for those of us remaining at the club after the holiday crowds have thinned, mid-winter can be a difficult time to sustain a commitment to fitness. It's hard to wake up and work out when the sun has yet to rise or to exercise after work, when it's already dark.

If you are someone whose resolve to exercise is giving way to the urge to hibernate, I hope this inspires you to hit the gym before hitting the couch.

Why exercise?
When you have a compelling reason to do something, you find ways to make it happen. If you've had trouble in the past sticking to an exercise program, perhaps it's time to reconsider your motivation. Acknowledge your private aspirations. Perhaps you'd like to be able to see your toes again, to feel attractive in a bathing suit, to have enough stamina to keep up with your grandchildren, or to live long enough to see if you will become a grandparent. You may find additional inspiration among the following list of exercise benefits. Once you've identified your motivators, remind yourself of them frequently. Let your motivation drown out any excuses.

Regular exercise can:

- add quality years to your life. Studies show that exercise improves longevity and helps prevent diseases such as cancer, Alzheimer's, and osteoporosis. According to a Harvard University study, one hour of vigorous exercise can add two hours to your life.[6]

- increase your metabolism. You probably know that exercise burns off calories and muscle burns more calories than fat. But did you also know that you continue to burn calories at a higher rate even after your workout, especially when your body has a higher ratio of muscle to fat?

- o promote muscle tone. Building muscles makes you stronger, increases endurance, and makes you look and feel better in a bathing suit.

- o increase bone density. Weight-bearing exercise will help increase bone density and prevent the bone loss that affects many post-menopausal women.

- o improve posture. Exercises that strengthen the abdominal muscles and torso promote good posture and support the back.

- o reduce injury. By strengthening the muscles and surrounding ligaments, joints are less prone to injury.

- o increase energy. Movement increases circulation and can often revive you more than a long winter's nap.

- o eliminate toxins. Exercise improves digestion. Working up a good sweat and drinking plenty of water will help flush out the system.

- o elevate mood. You don't have to be a marathoner to experience "runner's high." Endorphins are morphine-like chemicals released by the body during exercise that promote a feeling of well-being.

- o improve sleep. As long as you don't exercise too close to bedtime, you'll likely find it's easier to fall asleep, and you'll sleep more soundly.

- o reduce stress. Although it's best to deal with the source of stress, exercise is a healthy way to release tension and anxiety.

- o improve self-esteem. When you feel better about your body, you gain confidence and feel better about yourself in general.

Components of an exercise program
You should consult a doctor before launching into an exercise regimen. Many health clubs have personal trainers who will work with you to customize a fitness program. A good program will

include a mix of these three components:

1. Cardio-vascular or aerobic exercise (a minimum of three twenty-minute workouts a week): These activities raise your heart rate for a sustained period of time. My favorites include walking, running, hiking, biking, swimming, dancing, aerobics, cross-country skiing, and snow-shoeing. Other good options are rollerblading, kayaking, kickboxing, basketball, soccer, rock climbing, and ice-skating. Racquet sports, downhill skiing, and martial arts may not provide the same aerobic benefit because of frequent stops and starts, but they are still great fun and good exercise.

2. Stretching (in the beginning of every workout after warming up and at the end as you are cooling down): Stretching promotes flexibility, reduces muscle soreness, and prevents injury. Check out yoga as a way to get a different type of workout and to learn poses to incorporate in your stretching routine.

3. Strength training (two to three times a week): Strength training involves using weight or resistance as a way to build and tone muscles and increase bone density. Health clubs and gyms offer instruction on a wide range of weight equipment. You can strength train at home using push-ups, crunches, squats and purchased hand weights, balls, or bands. You may also want to look into Pilates as a way to condition the core of the body.

How to stick with it
Set yourself up for success by making sure to:

➢ choose wisely. It's critical to pick activities that you enjoy. If you have fun exercising, you are much more likely to make it a priority.

➢ cross-train. Vary your activities to work different muscle groups, prevent boredom, and minimize the risk of injury from over-use.

➢ experiment with different options to find out what works best for you. Do you like exercising first thing in the morning, during your lunch hour, when the baby naps, or before dinner? Do you prefer working out solo, with a friend, or in a group? Do you like to exercise indoors or outdoors, to music or in silence? Find what works and create those conditions.

- have a contingency plan. If you exercise outdoors, have a back up plan in case of inclement weather. Choose an exercise DVD, dance around the living room to your favorite music, or hop on a stationary bike with an exciting book.

- buddy up with an exercise partner. Having company helps to pass the time more quickly and makes exercising more fun. Being accountable to a partner can also help to keep you on track.

- reward yourself. Buy new workout clothes or treat yourself to a massage. If you have a health club membership, take full advantage of their amenities, i.e. hot tub, steam room, sauna, and personal training services.

- schedule your workouts as you would any other appointment. You'll be more likely to exercise if it's a commitment on your calendar and not something to squeeze in at the last minute.

- pace yourself and build up gradually. "Slow and steady wins the race" is a better motto to adopt than the outdated "No pain, no gain." An injury from overuse could set you back a few weeks or months.

- set a goal. Sign up for a race and devise a training schedule to prepare for it. Soliciting sponsors for a fundraising race will add extra incentive to your training.

A body at rest tends to stay at rest. A body in motion tends to stay in motion. So, get moving and make the law of inertia work for you, not against you!

~~~~~~

Resources:

When Working Out Isn't Working Out: A Mind/Body Guide to Conquering Unidentified Fitness Obstacles, by Michael Gerrish

The No Sweat Exercise Plan: Lose Weight, Get Healthy, and Live
~~~~~~

Longer (A Harvard Medical School Guide), by Harvey Simon

Yoga Shakti DVD, with Shiva Rea

Power Yoga for Beginners DVD, with Rodney Yee

Total Body Pilates DVD, by Karen Voight

Alpine Life Lessons

I think I've finally turned the corner with downhill skiing! In the past few years, I have improved both my technique and my confidence with an upgrade to new equipment and some instruction. I find I now begin runs with anticipation rather than apprehension. It's taken a while, but I'm finally developing a sense of rhythm. Occasionally, I'll even join my family on the more difficult black diamond trails.

Growing up in the South, I wasn't exposed to skiing until I moved to the Boston area in my late twenties. In contrast to my husband, who's been skiing since he was five years old, I had a lot of catching up to do. As I review what I've learned so far on the slopes, I realize that many of these principles apply to other areas of life. I share these lessons with you in hopes that they'll help you smoothly navigate the varied terrain of your life—curving slopes, fresh powder, icy patches, moguls, and all!

Find your way
We all make our way independently and often in very different manners. Some, like my daredevil sons, hurl themselves down the mountain at breakneck speed, enjoying the rush, skiing close to the trees, if not in the woods, to add to the challenge. Others, like me, meander more slowly, stopping occasionally to admire the scenery, carving large looping S's that give trees and other obstacles a wide berth. Find the pace and style that works for you.

Choose wisely
The #1 rule in skiing is to ski in control. This is to protect yourself and others. Know yourself and ski within your limits, pushing them occasionally to expand them. Make mindful choices about which trails to follow, when to let the skis run, when to carve a turn, and, most importantly, when to call it a day. Most ski injuries occur on the last run of the day, when the light is flat and legs are tired. Given the law of gravity, you are going to come down one way or the other. Your choices often determine whether you come down on your skis, on your behind, or on a ski patrol sled.

Pay attention
While skiing, you have to be aware of what's ahead, so you can make adjustments to avoid icy stretches or to catch some air on a jump. You also want to celebrate spectacular runs. To get the

most out of the experience, however, your attention needs to be, not in the future or the past, but in the here and now. On the chair lift, my mind and eyes wander, as I take in the mountain scenery and watch brightly outfitted skiers and snowboarders make their way down the mountain. When it's my turn on the trails, however, my focus is completely on the snow, my skis, my body, and the skiers right around me. Moments like this are mindfulness meditation in motion.

Be well equipped

For years I put up with boots that felt like vise grips. Getting into and out of them was torturous. I always badly bruised my big toenails, which later would turn purplish black and would inevitably fall off at the beginning of sandal season. Yuck! When I was fitted for new boots, I recall the salesperson commenting that my old boots were good ones but were ideal for those with narrow feet, not wide ones like mine. Technology can make things easier or create more of a struggle. Make sure you have the proper equipment and know how to use it.

Be resilient

One of the very first things they teach beginners is how to get back up from a fall. Falls are inevitable. Fortunately, they become less frequent, the more accomplished you become. What's important is that you are able to right yourself, brush off both snow and your wounded pride, and head back down the trail. Perseverance pays off.

Learn from others

You can improve your technique by observing how it's done, imitating, and eventually improvising, as you begin to synthesize and develop your own style. Watch the pros on TV, take lessons, and observe other skiers as you ride the chair lift. Mimic accomplished skiers, perhaps following someone down the trail, turning when they do. Eventually you'll develop your own natural rhythm and style.

Enjoy yourself

Skiing, like life, is meant to be enjoyed. If you find you are miserable—the light snow has turned to driving rain or pelting sleet, or temperatures drop and frostbite threatens—it's time for a change. Take a break by the fireplace in the lodge, or move on to the après ski experience. As you stretch your legs, warm up with a hot drink, and share the day's highlights with friends and family, enjoy the satisfying glow in your cheeks and the heavy tiredness in your legs. With all of the exertion and fresh air, you'll sleep well tonight. That's a good thing because tomorrow you'll have a chance to do it all over again.

~~~~~~

Resources:

Inner Skiing, by W. Timothy Gallwey

Skiing from the Head Down, by Leonard Loudis and W. Charles Lobitz
~~~~~~

Living Well

Once on our way home from a Vermont ski weekend, we stopped for gas at a service station that offered two welcome perks. What initially drew us in was the covered self-serve island. This kept the sloppy mix of snow and rain off my husband as he filled the tank. The added bonus was a set of speakers on the outside of the building broadcasting music. I'm not the biggest fan of country music, but I was a captive audience that day. I found myself listening intently to George Strait's catchy tune and poignant message: "There's a difference in living and living well." During our trip home, I reflected upon the distinction between living and living well. I invite you to spend some time doing the same.

How would you define living well? What first came to my mind, no doubt inspired by the frigid temperature, were scenes from glossy travel ads of idyllic tropical beaches and luxurious spas. But I quickly thought of some more accessible, low-cost examples of family and friends living well that we can take advantage of daily:

- my father, who settles into his lazy boy recliner with a sigh and an interesting library book
- friends who sit out on their deck every summer evening to watch the sun set
- my German host parents who have perfected the art of leisurely mealtimes (German: *gemutliches Essen*)
- a friend who makes a nightly ritual out of taking a bath by candlelight

As you think about your own life, what current evidence do you have that you live well? You might include things often taken for granted: your health, a good night's sleep, or the unconditional love of a pet. You may also consider more obvious indulgences: a fine bottle of wine, a decadent dessert, or silk lingerie. I hope the length of your initial list pleasantly surprises you.

How could you expand your list and move from living to consistently living well? There are many small steps that can make a big difference in your quality of life. A shift in thinking is one example. Instead of focusing on what's lacking in your life, use an affirmation such as "All is well. I live well." You'll soon begin believing it. What are things that you currently do (think eat, drink, sleep, bathe) that with more intention and attention could begin to feel like nurturing rituals instead of routines? What do you have access to but aren't currently taking advantage of that could contribute to living well? Here's a list to get you thinking:

- fine china
- candles
- music—to listen to or play
- babysitter
- comfy couch
- Jacuzzi
- skin lotion or massage oil
- yoga mat
- exercise videos/DVDs, exercise classes, or equipment
- unredeemed gift certificates
- bread machine
- crock pot
- fresh flowers

My challenge to you is to not "get through" the coming day, week, and month but to live it and live it well!

~~~~~~

Resources:

Simple Abundance: A Daybook of Comfort and Joy, by Sarah Ban Breathnach

Living a Beautiful Life: 500 Ways to Add Elegance, Order, Beauty and Joy to Every Day of Your Life, by Alexandra Stoddard
~~~~~~

Reconnecting

It's not a good feeling to be out of touch. The last time I moved my office, there was a period during which I could only sporadically maintain a connection to the Internet and send or receive emails. It was frustrating to hear from clients and friends that their emails had bounced back. I was worried and angry, wondering what important news or opportunity I might have missed.

In contrast, I've also had some wonderful experiences reconnecting with old friends and colleagues. For instance, one year after the holidays, I caught up with two dear friends from Virginia whom I've known since first grade but haven't seen in several years. A while back, my husband and I also attended a reunion of employees from the company where we met back in 1988. What fun it was to find out what everyone's doing now, to learn who'd become grandparents, and to discover that we weren't the only couple to break the "no dating or marrying" company policy. (Hey, some rules are worth breaking!) I had such fun renewing old acquaintances and friendships that I'm going to continue to reach out to others with whom I've lost contact.

Let the lingering spirit of Auld Lang Syne and the Valentine's Day celebrations of love inspire you to rekindle a romantic relationship, reunite with distant family members, and reconnect with old friends. Here are a few ideas for ways to reestablish and recharge connections:

- Pick up the phone and call someone whom you've been thinking of recently. Chances are if they've been popping into your mind, you've been on their mind as well.

- If you can't gather for a group hug, gather for a group call. There are now many telephone conferencing services such as www.freeconference.com or www.freeaudioconferencing.com that offer free bridge lines. You can enjoy a family reunion without having to leave home.

- Stay in touch by email. This works especially well across time zones. My sister, who is a night owl, lives on the West Coast. I'm an early riser who lives on the East Coast. Email makes it easy for us to communicate when we are both awake and alert.

- Use instant messaging for a virtual chat. Ask any teenager for a tutorial if you are not sure how to use this technology.

- Send a card or letter. As "snail mail" becomes less popular, it is even more treasured.

- Pass along interesting or humorous articles, quotes, and cartoons.

- Treat yourself and your spouse/significant other to a date night or getaway weekend.

- Do some Internet sleuthing to track down long lost friends and classmates. I know of at least one very happy pair of high school sweethearts who have reunited after finding each other on www.classmates.com.

- Organize a potluck or catered Dutch treat gathering for a group (from work, church, a sports team, or a playgroup).

- Create traditions of an annual block party, Yankee Swap, or progressive dinner party. In my sister-in-law and brother-in-law's neighborhood, they rotate hosting Friday night "Flamingo Nights." The plastic pink flamingos in the front yard let everyone know where the cocktail party is.

- Plan girls-only or boys-only outings to the movies, a museum exhibit, a spa, or sporting event. A night out is often easiest to schedule, but a day trip or weekend away is even more of a hoot.

- Set aside time for a weekly or bi-weekly coffee or lunch date that's not work-related. This is a great way to catch up with local friends.

- Plan a vacation with your extended family. Rent a beach house, book adjacent campsites, or stay at the same hotel or inn.

- Buy season's tickets to the theater, opera, symphony, or your favorite team's sporting events to guarantee regular nights out with your spouse or friend.

It's easy to get caught up in the busyness of work and family commitments, over time creating an insular existence. Yes, it does take effort to reconnect with others, but it is well worth it. Whom would you like to reach out to today?

Give it Time

During the winter, I like to make at least one big pot of soup a week. Making soup is not a process you can rush, but it is well worth the wait. It's not fast food or something you can quickly zap in the microwave. Most recipes call for the soup to simmer for at least an hour so the flavors of the broth, vegetables, and seasonings mellow and merge. Many soups, such as minestrone, lentil, or mushroom-barley are even better the next day. The soup thickens as it sits, enhancing the texture and the taste. Making soup is the perfect project for an at-home weekend afternoon. Once all the vegetables are chopped and the seasonings are added, it doesn't need a lot of tending, but it does need time.

Like soup, good things take time. This holds true for many of the endeavors my coaching clients are involved in: growing a business, writing a book, having a baby, buying a home, getting into shape, finding fulfilling work, developing relationships, and mastering new skills. Most would rather snap their fingers and instantly reach their goal, but it rarely happens that way. Here are some suggestions to make the waiting easier and to facilitate the process:

Hold and share your vision
Visualize the desired outcome. Create it first in your mind so that you can manifest it in your life. If you aren't sure exactly what you are looking for, for example, in a life partner or a new job, you are more likely to settle for less than a desirable match. When you get really clear about what you want, you exponentially increase your chances of getting it. Make wish lists, collages, or journal entries to help you bring what you want into focus. Once you've nailed down the specifics of what you want, share your vision with others, so they can contribute ideas, introductions, advice, referrals, and resources.

Take action
It's not easy to be patient. Being idle can make the wait feel like an eternity. It feels good to take even small steps toward your goal, whether it's setting up systems to handle more clients for a new business or preparing a nursery for a baby. Most final outcomes are reached through a number of smaller, incremental steps. Look for opportunities to pave the way for your dream. Recognize yourself for the efforts you are making, even if the reward hasn't yet materialized. The Stepping Stones exercise detailed in the "Beginnings" section can be an invaluable aid in

breaking long-term projects down into manageable, short-term objectives.

Give something away
Put the Universal Law of Karma to work for you. When you give with a generous heart, good things come back to you in return. Clear clutter and donate unwanted items to charity. This has the added benefit of creating space for new things to come into your life. Contribute to worthy causes. Volunteering your time and expertise is a great way to give when you are looking for a job or promoting a new business. It won't eat into your savings and can yield good visibility and contacts.

Allow yourself to be in the process
If you are only focused on the outcome, you'll miss out on valuable experiences along the way. Some of the best learning takes place during periods of transition. You may be a different person from the change and growth that takes place in the process. Even major setbacks, such as divorce or physical injury, create new strength and resiliency. A bone, for instance, becomes stronger after healing from a break.

Experiment with adding a few of these strategies to what's in your pot, give it time, and when at last it's time to announce, "Soup's on!" sit back and savor the delicious results.

Hold That Thought

Winter travel can be a nail-biting experience. It can also be an opportunity to put trust and the power of intention to the test. What happened on a recent February trip to the West Coast reinforced my belief that what we think about we bring about.

On the day of departure, I was scheduled on an 8:35 a.m. flight from Boston to Chicago, where I'd connect to a flight to Los Angeles. From there, I had a reservation for a shuttle van to take me to Long Beach, where I'd board a cruise ship and join the Coach U faculty for a four-day retreat. I was excited about meeting my fellow faculty members, going on my first cruise, and even having the travel time to read, write, and think. I'd allowed a cushion of time between each travel segment and felt confident that all would go smoothly.

The snow, predicted to be light flurries until mid-day, turned out to be quite heavy the morning of my trip. Before I left, I heard on the news that snow was falling at a rate of an inch an hour but that Boston's Logan airport was open. Although it wasn't ideal traveling weather, I wasn't worried. I'd received an email confirmation that my flight was on time, and despite constant complaints about the road conditions, my limo driver got me safely to the airport by 7:00 a.m. I was grateful that I decided not to drive myself to the airport as I usually do.

Since it was a school vacation week, I had a feeling that using the curbside check-in was the way to go, especially since the lines inside looked pretty long. The sky cap was a cheery young fellow, and I decided, as he went to the computer, that I'd tip him generously. When he came back, his smile was replaced by a serious expression. He told me my flight was cancelled. Many flights were cancelled since the storm was widespread, and lots of planes couldn't get to Boston in time for their scheduled departures. Lots of people were trying to reschedule. The sky cap said there were two flights going to L.A. that morning: a direct flight at 8:00 a.m. and one with a connection at 11:00 a.m. The later flight would require a connection and would get me to L.A. with very little time to spare to make it to the pier by the 4:30 p.m. boarding cut-off time. He told me to wait while he went back in to the ticket counter; he knew someone there who'd help out.

As I waited, shivering on the curb, I kept thinking about how wonderful it would be to get on the early flight. I could feel my pulse quicken as many negative thoughts beginning with "what if" and "why didn't" vied for my attention. "What if I couldn't get on the early flight? What if I got to L.A. after the boat left? Why didn't I purchase travel insurance? Why didn't I fly out a day or two early given the notoriously unpredictable New England weather? Why didn't I check the flight status one more time before I left?" Each time a negative thought popped into my mind, I stopped it and replaced it with the intention that I'd be enjoying warmer weather and the good company of colleagues by the end of the day. In my mind's eye, I pictured the sky cap returning with the news that I was booked on the early flight. He came back and told me he'd checked the bags on the 8:00 a.m. flight but that I'd have to fly standby. There were a few other standbys ahead of me, including a family of four, but if all four of them couldn't get on, then I could.

At the departure gate, I said a silent prayer and pictured myself boarding the flight and settling into my seat with a sigh of relief. I asked the gate attendant how promising it looked. He said both flights to L.A. were booked solid, so it was possible I wouldn't fly out that day. After another minute or two at the computer, he said he didn't want to get my hopes up too much, but there were a couple of people who hadn't checked in yet. I'd have to wait, and they'd call standbys if seats became available. I sat down to call my husband to let him know of the change in plans. I told him I thought I'd make the early flight and asked him to hold that intention for me as well. I chatted with the friendly businessmen around me. I told them I hoped to join them on the flight. I explained my situation and felt as if they were rooting for me, too. There was a delay, so the wait and boarding seemed to last forever. I ended up being the last standby—one of two—to get on the flight. Whew!! I arrived in L.A. with plenty of time to get to the boat, and it was smooth sailing for the rest of my trip.

I'm not sure if it was the sky cap pulling some strings, my lucky stars, my guardian angels working overtime, the power of my positive thinking, or some combination of the above that helped me get the last seat. I'm grateful for whatever worked. Some of the things I believe made a difference, which can be used in any type of stressful situation are:

Visualizing the outcome
I only allowed myself to picture myself getting to Los Angeles with plenty of time to spare.

Checking your thoughts
When I caught myself beginning to worry, I redirected my thoughts. Notice when you begin getting caught in the vortex of negative thinking. One bad thought easily leads to another. Our thoughts are powerful, so don't give negative ones any more fuel. Put the brakes on. You don't want to go there!

Trusting that all will work out for the best
Face it; things don't always go as planned. In hindsight, however, they do usually work out in our favor. For instance, the 8:00 a.m. flight that I ended up taking was a direct flight, an option that wasn't even available to me at the time I booked the trip.

Thoughts and intentions are powerful tools for manifestation. Don't miss the boat! Put yours to work for you today.

~~~~~~

Resources:

Change Your Thoughts Change Your Life, by Wayne Dyer

Dr. Norman Vincent Peale: Three Complete Books: The Power of Positive Thinking: The Positive Principle Today; Enthusiasm Make the Difference, by Dr. Norman Vincent Peale
~~~~~~

Snow Day: Another Miracle of Manifestation

Listening to winter weather reports reminds me of a time one January when meteorologists were forecasting a big snowstorm for the following day. So far that winter there had not yet been any school cancellations. Oh, how my sons were wishing for a snow day! My older son, who was almost fourteen, had heard that if you wear pajamas inside out you'll get a snow day. He came downstairs that evening with pockets flapping and the skiers on his flannel pajamas no longer visible—they were facing inside.

At 6:15 a.m. the next morning, peering into the pre-dawn darkness, we saw no snow on the ground and only a few flakes falling. Seeing my son's crestfallen face, I suggested that we turn on the TV news to get the latest update. The weatherman was still calling for around a foot of snow in our area, beginning in the morning and lasting most of the day. There were lots of school closings scrolling on the bottom of the screen. We watched, holding our breath, until they finally reached our town and we saw "Closed." I wish I'd had a camera handy to capture the look on my son's face as he exclaimed, "It worked! We have a snow day!"

Soon after this we watched the movie *What the Bleep Do We Know!?,* which explains the "magical" power of thought and energy in terms of quantum physics. Later we all watched *The Secret*, which demystifies the Law of Attraction, the principle of like attracting like, also called the Law of Magnetism. Although I've been studying and discussing manifestation and the Law of Attraction with my family for years, he's at the age where he rolls his eyes and probably thinks, "What the bleep does she know!?" when I bring up such topics. Having, however, his ski team coach show *The Secret* during a recent practice was enough to grab his attention. Between all of these experiences, I think my son has begun to grasp that we really do create our own reality.

In case manifestation piques your interest as well, here's a basic outline of steps in the process:

1. **Desiring**

The process often begins with dissatisfaction, an observation of something that's less than ideal, and clarity about what it is that you do want and why you want it. This desire becomes a request.

From a spiritual perspective, you might think of it as placing an order with the Universe, making a prayer of petition, or calling upon your angels and guides for help.

2. **Thinking**
If your desire is motivated by lack or fear, it's important to reframe it as a positive thought, since what we think about, whether positive or negative, is what we bring about. In my son's case, an initial desire "for school to be closed tomorrow" focuses on school and is better reframed as "I want a snow day," focusing on snow. You also must believe in the possibility of what you want coming true. You have to expect miracles before they can happen. One technique at this stage is to create a mental picture of your desired outcome.

3. **Feeling**
As much as I endorse affirmations, thoughts alone may not be enough to make your dreams come true. Combine your thoughts with positive feelings, however, and you'll put the Law of Attraction to work for you. Let yourself steep in the feelings of euphoria, excitement, or peace that you'll have when you get what you desire. The higher vibration created by the energy of these feelings becomes a powerful magnet, pulling what you want your way.

4. **Receiving**
This final stage is about being open to, but not forcing, an outcome. It's also not a passive process; you don't want to watch opportunities pass by you. Instead, take advantage of doors that open for you by taking appropriate action. For instance, follow through by contacting a referral that someone gives you, or check out a recommended resource.

I encourage you to experiment with this process, whether you apply it to New Year's Resolutions or to snow days. May it help you create just what you want in life.

~~~~~~

Resources:

The Secret, by Rhonda Byrne

Ask and It is Given and other books by Jerry and Esther Hicks
~~~~~~

Spring

Stuck: A Metaphor of Mud and Snow

Have you ever been stuck? Ever been in a rut that you couldn't seem to get out of despite your best efforts? Ever felt that the harder you tried, the more it seemed like you were spinning your wheels, burying yourself deeper? A friend of mine once found herself, quite literally, in this situation. As she backed down my steep driveway in a snowstorm, ironically on the first official day of spring, her car slipped into and became stuck in my garden. Through her story, I hope that you'll find strategies to apply to difficult situations in your own life.

Assess the situation
Her car was in a tough spot. There was a small boulder to the right of the car and a boxwood shrub to her left. Our mailbox was two feet behind her, and her front tires were dug so far into the snow that the nose of her car was level with the ground. The only way out appeared to be the way she'd come in. This would require moving up the slope, onto the driveway and trying to back up again.

Ask for help
Fifteen or twenty minutes must have passed between when I said goodbye to my friend and the moment I realized she was stuck. It was past my boys' bedtime, so it wasn't until after reading to them and tucking them in that I looked out of the window to see if it was still snowing. That's when I saw her car's lights in the garden. She'd been going it alone, attempting to move forward but was only becoming more deeply mired in the snow and dirt. She hadn't wanted to disturb me, but clearly, extricating the car was more than a one-person job.

Look at what you have going for you
We had some tools at our disposal: shovels, some sand and a blanket for traction, and people I could ask to push if needed. Since we'd both had some experience with cars in snow, we decided to first go with what we knew best.

Clear the way
To free up her wheels, we first dug out the snow that was packed tightly between her front tires and the rim of the car. We also cleared away the snow in front of and in back of her tires.

Use an incremental approach
In our initial attempt, we spread sand in front of the tires. We

hoped that would give her tires something to grip onto, so she could slowly work her way out of the garden.

Be willing to abandon plans
When shoveling and sanding didn't make a bit of difference, we knew we had to take another tack. My husband was just finishing a business call, so I asked for his assistance.

Explore different options
Instead of fighting an uphill battle, my husband suggested removing the mailbox and backing out onto the street. My friend and I were working from the assumption that the mailbox was a fixed obstacle. Not so! Since it had never been cemented in, it easily lifted out.

Create movement
Even though the plan was go backward, moving slightly forward and then backward to create a rocking motion is what finally made the car budge. It's counterintuitive to move in a different direction that you want to go, but often *any* sort of movement is enough to get things rolling.

Give a good push to keep it going
Once the car started to move, a few strong pushes helped send it on its way.

Everything turned out fine. My friend made it safely home. My garden escaped remarkably unscathed—the only plants affected were the mums that I pull out every spring anyway. Since she's not the only friend who has done battle with our driveway, we now offer a valet service.

I hope one or more of these approaches come in handy the next time you are feeling stuck in mud, snow, or life.

~~~~~~~~~~~~~~~~~~~~~~~~~~~~~~~~~~~~~~~

Resources:

Getting Unstuck Without Coming Unglued: Restoring Work-Life Balance, by Sharon Teitelbaum
~~~~~~~~~~~~~~~~~~~~~~~~~~~~~~~~~~~~~~~

Sleep Soundly

What a difference a good night's sleep makes! It's much easier to feel balanced when I wake up refreshed and in good spirits. I find that enough hours of sound sleep fortify me with the resilience to meet whatever the day offers. When I haven't slept well, I'm apt to be cranky and impatient. My energy lags and it's difficult to get through the afternoon without a nap. Although I stick to herbal tea, when I'm sleep-deprived I can understand how "hi-test" coffee and tea drinkers rely on a boost from a few cups of their favorite brew.

As a light sleeper, I find it can be a challenge to always sleep well. In the warmer months when we sleep with the windows wide open, the birds make a ruckus at 4:30 or 5:00 a.m., waking me long before my ideal eight hours of sleep. Sometimes I get back to sleep, but not always. Travel can also throw off my sleep schedule. It often takes me longer to fall asleep in a strange bed, and noises I'm not accustomed to wake me up in the night.

If you watch television, you've undoubtedly seen commercials advertising the pills pharmaceutical companies would love you to take whenever you have trouble sleeping. But before asking your doctor for a prescription, I encourage you to explore other ways to sleep soundly.

Create a soothing sleep environment
Choose calming colors and patterns when you decorate your bedroom. Minimize clutter to create a tranquil setting. Choose something beautiful and uplifting, such as a lovely painting or a photo of your beloved, to be the last thing you see before you shut your eyes.

Make a cozy bed
Everyone has their personal preference when it comes to firmness of mattress, type of pillow, thread count of sheets, and weight of blankets. If you travel or are an overnight guest in someone's home, pay attention to how you sleep with different bedding. As you age your preferences may change. If you wake up feeling stiff, a softer mattress, a feather bed, or an egg crate mattress pad may help.

Keep cool
I like fresh, cool air when I sleep and prefer to sleep with open windows in the warm months and a cracked window during

the winter. Especially if you suffer from occasional hot flashes, sleeping in a room that's too warm may interrupt your sleep. A hot bath or a hot tub can be very relaxing before bed, but make sure you've given yourself plenty of time to cool down before going to bed.

Block out distractions

Ear plugs, a white noise machine, room darkening blinds, and a satin eye mask can all prevent light and noise from jarring your senses and disturbing your slumber.

Create boundaries around your bed

Don't worry, I'm not suggesting that you create a moat around your bed, but I do recommend keeping the TV out of the bedroom. Sleep experts recommend that you reserve your bed for sleeping and making love so that there's a conditioned, Pavlovian relaxation response when you get into bed. You also don't want to associate your bed with tossing and turning, so if you wake up and can't get back to sleep after twenty minutes or so, get up and go into another room. You can read something (choose something dull, not an exciting novel) or drink some hot milk or chamomile tea.

Practice good sleep habits

Go to bed and get up at the same times. If you've ever experienced jet lag, you know what it's like to have your circadian rhythms disrupted. Do your best to stick to a regular bedtime, even on weekends or on vacation.

Treat the source, not the symptom

Identify what's interfering with a sound sleep, and seek relief for the root cause. Whether pain, anxiety, over-stimulation, or your partner's snoring is the culprit, it's better to handle the root cause of the problem than to only treat your sleeplessness.

Avoid stimulants and alcohol

Shy away from anything that's over stimulating or upsetting before bedtime. Caffeine, a heavy or spicy meal, vigorous exercise, and violent images may kick your body into a higher gear at a time when you want to downshift. Although alcohol does have a sedative effect, beware the fallacy of the nightcap. After drinking alcohol, many people wake up a few hours after going to sleep because they are thirsty (alcohol dehydrates), they have to go to the bathroom, or because the sugar in the alcohol makes their blood sugar plummet.

Relax
Look for ways to wind down before retiring. Once you get into bed, there are numerous ways to promote relaxation. Sex is a wonderful sedative. You can do progressive relaxation exercises in which you relax one part of your body at a time. You can listen to soothing music or follow a guided relaxation or visualization. There are tonal recordings that help you access different brainwave states. I've found the Silva Ultramind System www.silvaultramind.com very effective for reaching the alpha, meditative state. Tom Kenyon's *Deep Rest* available from www.soundstrue.com ushers you into a low delta, deeply relaxed state.

Turn to a natural sleep aid when needed
If you occasionally need help falling asleep, there are a number of natural remedies that can help. Our whole family has found Bach Flower Rescue Sleep remedy to be effective. I've fallen asleep a few times during the final relaxation in yoga class after receiving a spritz from a lavender aromatherapy spray. The one time my back went out, my chiropractor gave me some tablets containing the herb valerian, which is a relaxant. Please be aware that some herbs and supplements may interfere with medications or be contraindicated. Ask your doctor, a naturopath, or herbalist for recommendations.

Recognize the power of a nap
At times a nap can be lifesaving. My husband once caught himself nodding off behind the wheel. After a short nap at the next rest stop, he was then alert enough to drive himself and our then infant son safely home. A brief nap—twenty minutes is ideal—can help you deal with a sleep deficit. It can recharge you and make the rest of the day more productive and enjoyable. But naps can sometimes sabotage a good night's sleep. A rule of cognitive-behavioral therapy for insomnia, or CBT-I, is to stay awake, restricting sleep during the day so you can stay asleep at night. Discover how your body responds, and make smart choices about napping.

May these approaches help you easily fall and stay asleep so that you catch all the zzz's you need.

~~~~~~

Resources:

www.cbtforinsomnia.com—Learn more about short-term
~~~~~~

cognitive-behavioral therapy for insomnia.

www.centers.sleepfoundation.org—Get general information and locate a sleep center near you.

www.womentowomen.com—You can take a short assessment to see if your sleep problems are hormonally related.

www.silvaultramind.com—Download several free relaxations and alpha sound recordings, and learn about their training.

www.bachquiz.com—Learn more about Bach flower remedies and find your personal remedy.

Go with the Flow

Spring takes its time coming to New England. As it approaches, the brighter light and warming temperatures create a "spring surge" of energy in me. During a two-week span one spring, in addition to my normal activities, I developed a conference proposal, updated a brochure, organized my books and the playroom, cleaned the pantry and refrigerator, planned a summer trip to several Southwestern National Parks, started seeds inside, cleared my garden, picked up trash in my neighborhood, planned my son's birthday party, had two evenings out with my husband and friends, and read a great book. I was really on a roll! And I swear that I don't use caffeine! I'd like to share some ways to work with your natural flow of energy to have more fun and be more productive.

Facilitate flow
What gets your creative juices flowing? What makes you feel in sync with the world around you? There are many practices, which I describe on my website in my the Spirit section of my blog www.balancewithgrace.com/blog that can help you create and maintain a connected state. Yoga, Tai Chi, Qi Gong, and meditation are a few that combine body awareness and/or movement with focused breathing to help you work with your energetic flow. Discover what allows you to access and harness your energy, and practice regularly.

Prioritize based on preferences
Pay attention to what you are compelled to do and when you are drawn to certain activities. If you schedule activities based on when you most enjoy them, that's when you'll be most productive. For instance, I am inspired to tidy up in the morning. After the kids get on the school bus and before I start my work day, I scurry around, cleaning up the kitchen, putting clothes away, and making my bed. It takes me twice as long to pick up in the evening before bed.

Schedule strategically
Do tasks that require a high level of concentration when you're at your energy peak. Reserve activities that require a low level of concentration for times when you aren't as sharp. For instance, since I'm a morning person, I schedule business activities that need high and medium levels of concentration during the morning and early afternoon. Low level tasks work best for me in the afternoon. For example:

High: coaching, teaching, writing, creating programs, planning
Medium: taking classes, networking, responding to email, doing research and follow-up
Low: updating database, sorting, filing, organizing email

Women: honor the cycles of Nature.

A few years ago, I noticed that I often came down with colds around the time of my period. After learning more about the female cycle in Christiane Northrup's book, *Women's Bodies, Women's Wisdom,* I now intentionally slow down at that time and rarely get sick. Women are naturally more outgoing and energetic in the follicular phase of their menstrual cycle, between their periods and ovulation. This is a great time to initiate new projects, create, and socialize. Mental and emotional creativity peaks at ovulation. The luteal phase, the two weeks or so leading up to menstruation, is conducive for reflection and inward focus. Intuition is heightened and there's a natural ebb of energy. This is a great time for planning, writing, and doing more administrative or menial tasks. With the onset of their periods, many women feel a need to clean, clear clutter, and create order.

Give it a whirl and see what happens when you work with your energy and go with the flow. You may be amazed at the results!

~~~~~~

Resources:

www.drnorthrup.com—Christiane Northrop's site focuses on women's health issues and the inextricable relationship of spiritual and physical well-being.

The Power of Full Engagement: Managing Energy, Not Time, Is the Key to High Performance and Personal Renewal, by Jim Loehr and Tony Schwartz

Eight Simple Qigong Exercises for Health, by Dr. Yang, Jwing-Ming

Flow: The Psychology of Optimal Experience, by Mihaly Csikszentmihalyi
~~~~~~

Oh DEAR!

Once, in looking through my son's homework folder, a bright green bookmark caught my eye. These bookmarks had been given to all the children to help build awareness of and increase participation in D.E.A.R. Day, which is April 12. DEAR stands for Drop Everything And Read. What a great concept and holiday! Please join me in celebrating it. If you are not already in the habit of reading regularly, here are a few reasons that might convince you to D.E.A.R.

Reading provides a welcome escape
Reading, especially reading fiction, is a fabulous stress reliever because it plucks you out of your immediate circumstances, transporting you into another time, place, and situation. I notice that reading helps me wind down more easily in the evenings. Great fiction contributes to my feeling completely refreshed and recharged after weekends or vacations. Recommendation: *The Time Traveler's Wife*, by Audrey Niffennegger, or *The Earthsea Cycle*, by Ursula LeGuin.

Reading expands your mind
Books allow you to explore the world and learn about a multitude of topics without ever leaving home. Especially if you are a visual learner, reading is a wonderful way to absorb information. If you are an auditory learner or struggle with reading, audio books may work well for you. Recommendation: Ken Wilbur's *Kosmic Consciousness* audio program.

Reading sets a good example
Children mimic adult role models. If your children frequently see you read, whether its books, magazines, or newspapers, they are more apt to become avid readers. This certainly has held true in our household. When my younger son was a fifth-grader, he read two or three books a week and set an ambitious goal to read a hundred books in a year. If your children are young, reading aloud to them is a wonderful way to instill a love of reading. For preschoolers I'd recommend any of the many picture books from Leo Leoni or Eric Carle. The *Harry Potter* series, by J. K. Rowling, is a hit with school-age children.

Reading expands your capacity for compassion
Books provide an opportunity to briefly view life through the eyes of a person of another sex, ethnicity, nationality, culture, or era. Your particular set of problems and challenges may pale in

comparison to those of the characters in the book. This can help you become more empathetic towards others and more grateful for your own life. Recommendations: *Memoirs of a Geisha*, by Arthur Golden and *The Curious Incident of the Dog in the Night-Time,* by Mark Haddon.

Some of my favorite fiction writers include: Gail Tsukiyama, Jodi Picoult, Barbara Kingsolver, Amy Tan, Sue Monk Kidd, Kaye Gibbons, Margaret Atwood, Penelope Lively, Khaled Hosseini, Tracy Chevalier, Maeve Binchy, Dan Brown, and P.D. James. Other all-time favorite books of mine are Anita Diament's *The Red Tent,* and Wally Lamb's *She's Come Undone*.

When you do decide to D.E.A.R., may your book selection delight you and quickly works its magic. Happy reading!

Money Matters

Money. It's one of those tricky topics. It's on people's minds but isn't often frankly discussed. But let's face it: money matters. We are living in a time of economic uncertainty. Investors watch their portfolios with queasy stomachs, employees complain of paltry or nonexistent pay raises, and the unemployed continue to pound the pavement. If you, like many, are currently worried about finances, here are some steps to take to feel more in control of your money. As I'm not a financial professional, this is not meant as expert advice. These are simply things I've learned over the years from books, conferences, and personal experience that can minimize financial stress.

Examine your views, beliefs, and fears around money
Your mindset may be holding you back. Do you think money is a tool, an energy exchange, or the root of all evil? Here's a simple exercise that can be quite revealing. Make three columns, one for your dad on the left, one for your mom on the right, and one for you in the middle. In your parents' columns, record what you recall them doing, saying, or believing about money. Then fill in your own. Your column may be a reflection or a combination of your parents'. It may be the complete opposite. Decide which of your current beliefs you would like to keep and which ones you are you now ready to discard.

Know how much you are worth
Ignorance is not always bliss. In fact, uncertainty can cause as much, if not more, stress than seeing the bottom line. Calculate your net worth by subtracting your liabilities—debt and expenses—from your assets—cash, savings, equity or property. What assets could you liquidate easily and without penalty if you needed cash?

Know where your money goes
Figure out what you typically spend in a month. Keep a detailed record of your spending for the next week or month, including how you spend cash withdrawn from ATMs. Consider using accounting software, which forces you to categorize expenses. Some credit card companies also offer annual itemized statements, which can help you keep tabs on your spending.

Live within your means
If your income isn't enough to meet your monthly expenses, you basically have two choices: spend less or make more. On the spending side, figure out ways to trim non-essentials. How much money do you spend on things you want compared with things you truly need? On the earning side, are there ways to earn extra money through overtime, moonlighting, or passive revenue sources?

Be financially responsible
Look at where you are being financially irresponsible and take corrective action. Examples of financial irresponsibility include: ignoring bank statements, paying bills and/or taxes late, living beyond your means, charging items you can't afford, not paying off credit cards, not investing for the future, and avoiding difficult money discussions.

Establish an emergency reserve fund
Most experts recommend that you keep a buffer of three to six months of living expenses in a readily accessible interest-earning account. It's easy to scoff at this recommendation, thinking you'd never need access to that amount of money. We once had a scare, thinking we'd have to sink $20,000 into repairing our septic system. If we'd had we had a robust reserve this might not have been so worrisome. (Luckily, we later got the all clear signal. Whew!)

Know whom to turn to for expert advice
It's reassuring to have a team of experts including an accountant/tax expert, financial planner or advisor, and a lawyer who does estate planning. When choosing financial professionals, ask for referrals and get references. Research their credentials as well as their investment track record. Find out if any complaints have been filed against them.

Educate yourself about money
Even with a team of experts, you are still the one responsible for your money. Never make an investment that you don't fully understand.

Be well protected
Carry adequate health, life, disability, auto, and homeowners or renters insurance. Even if you are a stay-at-home parent and don't have your own income, if you have children who rely on you for care, insurance can help ensure that your children's needs

will be met, should anything happen to you.

Invest in the future by paying yourself first
The most painless way to save, if your employer offers a plan, is to set up an automatic payroll deduction to put 10% of every paycheck into savings. If you're self-employed, you'll need to discipline yourself to do this. Start as early as possible to take advantage of the power of compounding interest. Take full advantage of 401K plans, IRAs or SEPs. You'll save on taxes and feel more secure about your financial future.

Wealth is measured, not by how much money you make, but by how much money you keep and by the quality of your life. May you always use money wisely to create the life you want.

~~~~~~

Resources:

The Road to Wealth, The 9 Steps to Financial Freedom, by Suze Orman

Rich Dad, Poor Dad, and *The Cash Flow Game,* by Robert Kiyosaki

Dynamic Laws of Prosperity, by Catherine Ponder

Think and Grow Rich, by Napoleon Hill

How to Get Out of Debt, Stay Out of Debt, and Live Prosperously, by Jerrold Mundis

The Wall Street Journal Lifetime Guide to Money, edited by C. Frederic Wiegold
~~~~~~

Let the Games Begin

It's a good thing that the Winter Olympics only come along every four years because my family and I are practically glued to the TV for the duration of the games. My boys especially enjoy the snowboarding and the daredevil aerial maneuvers. My husband, a ski racer in his college years, gets his vicarious thrills watching the Men's Combined and Giant Slalom. As someone who's never even learned to skate backwards, I marvel at the artistry of the figure skaters and ice dancers. Once the Olympics are over, however, the TV gets more of a rest and we get back into playing our own games.

Most of us could benefit from watching less TV. Limiting violent TV shows and disturbing late-night news may reduce stress and improve sleep quality. Ever complain that there's not enough time or that there's too much to do? The average American could easily "find" an hour or two a day by turning off the TV. Evening is a natural time to slip into slower gear. But downtime doesn't have to be synonymous with Prime Time. There are many screen-free ways to unwind: working on a hobby or craft, playing a musical instrument, learning a language, reading, stargazing, and my all-time favorite—playing games.

We live in such a goal-oriented, production-driven society that it may seem like a frivolous waste of time to play games. That's nonsense! I view play as an integral part of a balanced life. I think my grandmother, who, by the way, lived to ninety-six, instilled this in me from the hours we spent playing Spite and Malice. Playing games brings back good memories. I can vividly picture the sunny breakfast nook where we played and her wrinkled hands as they dealt the cards. When my family plays games, I like to think of the memories we are creating for our children.

Playing games also promotes relaxation and encourages communication. Games provide the mental gymnastics to keep aging minds sharp and are a fun way for children to learn. Through our marathon Monopoly matches over the years, for example, my sons have developed math skills and learned the nuances of negotiating.

Games provide good, cheap fun. If you are thrifty you can trade games with a neighbor, scout out yard sales and the toy aisle of discount retailers like Marshalls or TJ Maxx, or request games for presents.

Here are some of our family's favorite games:

Board	Card	Dexterity
Mancala	Solitaire	Labyrinth
Blokus	Spite and Malice	Jacks
Backgammon	Go Fish	Pick Up Sticks
Cadoo	Rummy	Jenga
Parcheesi	War	Mikado
Yatzhee	Five Crowns	
*Monopoly	Quiddler	
*Scrabble	Set	
*Clue	Poker	
Chess	Cribbage	
Checkers	Old Maid	
Dominoes	Spit	
Scattagories	Pit	
Rummikub	Oh Sh*t!	
Quarto		

* You may prefer the Junior version of this game if you have young children.

Instead of settling down with the remote control, experiment with at least one "game night" this week. Ask your spouse, a friend, or your family to join you for a round or two of your favorite game. If you start now, you'll be well prepared for TV-free week, coming up the last week of April.

Earth Day Everyday

An often overlooked aspect of balance is living in harmony with the environment. In celebration of Earth Day on April 22, many communities sponsor activities to heighten awareness of the environment and the role each of us plays in preserving it. Each spring my family and I participate in a town-wide clean-up effort. We don heavy gardening gloves and set out with buckets and trash bags to clean up a nearby portion of state forest that borders a busy street. This quarter-mile stretch seems to be a magnet for bottles, cans, cigarette butts, and fast food wrappings. We are always amazed by how much we accumulate in a short time. We throw away the trash. If the recyclables aren't too dirty, we clean and bring them to the recycling area of our public works department, since we collect far more than what would fit in our curbside recycling bins. Afterwards, it is so rewarding to pass by and admire the pristine woods.

Unfortunately, it doesn't stay clean for long. Within a few days, I often spot several new cans and wrappers as I walk or jog by. I'll stop on my way back to collect yet another handful of trash. This makes me realize that it's not enough to do an annual clean-up blitz on Earth Day. To really make a difference, we need to think of every day as Earth Day. Here are some practices we can adopt to be better stewards of our environment:

Reduce

If you've recently gone for a walk or a drive on a trash collection day, I think you'll agree that we produce a staggering amount of garbage. There's a disposable version of most consumer goods: contacts lenses, razors, grocery bags, paper plates, plastic utensils, juice boxes, and even disposable cutting boards.

Before you make a purchase, ask yourself whether the item you are considering is necessary, how long it will last, and whether it is over-packaged. Consider using cloth napkins, canvas bags for your groceries, reusable plastic containers for sandwiches, and refillable bottles for water and juice. Single serving packages are convenient but create more waste than buying in bulk. Scale back on what you throw away. You'll probably be pleasantly surprised by how much money you'll save in the process.

Reuse
Before you throw something out, think if there is someone else who could use the item. There are many organizations that welcome donations of clothes, shoes, furniture, household items, computers, books, toys, bikes, and even cars! One man's trash can be another's treasure.

Recycle
Educate yourself about what's recyclable in your area, and take full advantage of curbside and town recycling. Bottles, cans, plastic milk containers, and paper—including newspaper, magazines, and junk mail—all belong in the recycling bin, not the trash. From my observations, many people don't realize that corrugated cardboard boxes, egg cartons, and cereal boxes can also be recycled. You may have to take some items to designated recycling bins at a local dump or public works department.

Detox
Pollutants are taking a toll on our air, water, soil, and health. There are effective and safe alternatives to pesticides and chemical lawn and garden products. Sprinkling or mulching with compost and leaving short grass clippings on your lawn are just two natural landscaping strategies. Inside the home, you can choose non-toxic cleaning supplies. On the Internet you can find many recipes using common pantry staples such as vinegar, salt, and baking soda to replace many household cleaners. Also, learn what items are considered hazardous waste, and find out how to properly dispose of them. An extensive list of household items, including computer and TVs, which contain cathode ray tubes, oil-based paint, motor oil, mercury thermometers, and some batteries, should not be put in the trash.

Compost
Ever noticed how quickly a banana peel turns brown? Compost happens! Invest in a low-cost black plastic compost bin, place it in a sunny spot, and regularly toss in layers of your non-meat and non-dairy food scraps: fruit and vegetable rinds, peels, eggshells, coffee filters and grounds, along with grass clippings, pulled weeds, leaves, and pet hair. In a few months you will have what gardeners refer to as "black gold." You can speed up the process by turning the compost pile, keeping it as moist as a damp sponge, and adding a few layers of finished compost and/or manure to the mix.

Purchase wisely
With every dollar you spend on organic foods, locally grown foods, or items made of recycled material, such as fleece, which is made from recycled plastic, you are casting a vote for the environment. Look for the recycling symbol—the triangle of three arrows—and select items that can be recycled or are made from post-recycled materials.

Conserve
Given this year's abundant spring rains, our town likely won't impose a water ban this summer. Even so, it's important to conserve our limited natural resources. Installing low-flow shower heads, toilet dams, using a rain barrel, and not over watering lawns (anything over one inch per week is excessive) are some ways to save water. You can save a substantial amount of electricity and money by replacing incandescent light bulbs with compact florescent bulbs. You can also save gas by carpooling, using public transportation, consolidating errands, and driving a fuel-efficient vehicle.

Clean up
We all share this planet. If we all pick up after ourselves it will make a difference. Go the extra mile and pick up after others, too. Bring a plastic bag with you on your next walk or hike, and collect some litter. Eventually, it may catch on.

So, if you see someone bending down by the side of the road, don't panic! It's probably me or an inspired reader picking up trash. Wish us well, and if you are able, join us!

~~~~~~

Resources:

www.earthday.org—Learn about ways to help on Earth Day (and everyday).

Animal, Vegetable, Miracle: A Year of Food Life, by Barbara Kingsolver
~~~~~~

Spring Cleaning for the Soul

Do you hesitate to invite friends over because your house is a mess? Do you cringe when you look at the inside of your car, purse, or pantry? Do you have a closet or cupboard that attacks when you open it? Can you easily find things in your home and office? If you answered no to any or all of these questions, perhaps it's time to consider Spring Cleaning.

First, let me set the record straight, I'm no perfectionist when it comes to housekeeping. This time of year especially, I'd rather be out in the garden. But I've learned that, just as we clear away leaves and prune the dead wood from plants and shrubs to encourage new growth, cleaning and clearing clutter from our homes is an effective way to free up energy and make room for new possibilities in our lives. I've found that it feels great to periodically weed out clutter and organize closets, cupboards, and drawers.

Clearing clutter is an exercise in letting go. The process of cleaning and clearing, while physically tiring, can at the same time be energizing. Paring down to the essentials is movement toward simplicity. There's a sense of peace and serenity that comes from restoring order to our surroundings. When we clear, we create space. Nature abhors a vacuum, so by creating space in our physical environment, we pave the way for something new to come our way. This doesn't mean that our physical space will necessarily be filled by another object; it could result in a new opportunity in a totally different area of our lives. It sounds rather hocus pocus, but I've seen too many examples with my clients and in my own life to believe otherwise. I don't think it's a coincidence that a big interview is landed after the apartment's overhauled, two new clients appear after the pantry's been cleaned, or the request for the summer off is approved days after the attic is organized.

Here are some spring cleaning strategies to inspire action:

When in doubt, throw it out
If you haven't worn or used something for the past six months to a year, you've obviously done quite well without it. If you have pack rat tendencies, which I confess, I do (everything seems to have art project potential), box up any items in question. If you still don't use them within the next three to six months, toss them. You'll never miss them when they're gone.

File a pile
If I'm feeling overwhelmed or unfocused, one of the quickest ways for me to feel centered again is to get rid of the mail pile that accumulates on my kitchen island. If you are feeling scattered at work, file away papers, and clear your desk to help regain clarity.

Reduce
Once you begin creating space, don't fill it with more unneeded stuff. To keep the mail pile from building back up, go to www.newdream.org, and select campaigns to generate letters that will get your name off mailing and telemarketing lists. Think twice before buying. Take advantage of your local library. You can borrow books, DVDs, CDs, CD-Roms, and in some towns even paintings.

Reuse
Pass outgrown clothes and toys on to relatives or friends. You'll feel good to get rid of your stuff, and they'll be pleased with the hand-me-downs. Local charities, shelters, and food pantries usually welcome donations. You could also turn this into a profitable experience by taking items to a consignment store or having a yard sale.

Recycle
Are you a box collector or a magazine and catalog hoarder? There's no need to save a product's box beyond its warranty period. Corrugated cardboard boxes, paperboard cereal boxes, and magazines can all be recycled. Put them out with your recycling or take them to the dump.

Find a place for everything
Train yourself and family members to put items back into place when they aren't being used. If organizing isn't your forte, consider hiring a personal organizer. The website for the National Association of Professional Organizers is www.napo.net.

Read up on it
If you are a person who likes to read about something before you jump into it, then you're in luck because there are lots of good books on cleaning and organizing. My tried and true favorites are listed below.

Invest in organizers
Purchase tiered shelving for your pantry, a double rod for your closet, or whatever it takes to keep items organized and easily accessible.

Schedule regular cleanouts
My children have learned that in order to make room for new birthday and Christmas presents, they need to part with some of their old toys. Just as children outgrow their toys, adults outgrow their stuff as well. Especially if you are growing through personal development work or coaching, be sure to update your surroundings to reflect who you are becoming, not where you have been.

Make a game of it
Set a timer for fifteen minutes once a day, and see how much you can do in that time. You may be so pleased with your progress that you decide to go for another round.

Reward yourself for your hard work.
Treat yourself to take-out. Sit back, and enjoy your orderly surroundings. Put your feet up while relaxing with a good novel, or take a nice long bath.

~~~~~~

Resources:

Clear Your Clutter with Feng Shui, by Karen Kingston

Clutter Control, by Jeff Campbell

Organizing from the Inside Out, by Julie Morgenstern

It's Hard to Make a Difference if You Can't Find Your Keys, by Marilyn Paul
~~~~~~

Chaos and Order

Have you ever been so struck by a word or concept that a speaker introduced that you sat bolt upright and hung on to every word? That's how I felt during a recent coaching conference session when the presenter, master coach and author, C. J. Hayden, used and defined the word "chaord." This is a term—the combination of chaos and order—that was coined by Dee W. Hock and is detailed in his book *Birth of the Chaordic Age*. The notion of the simultaneous existence of chaos and order appealed to me because, with the exception of that brief period immediately after our housecleaners come and before my boys return from school, my home is rarely completely in order. It's also never in absolute chaos. It is in the realm of chaord.

Since being introduced to the chaordic concept, it doesn't bother me if my desk becomes temporarily cluttered with papers or there are pots and pans and ingredients all over my kitchen counters. Creation is naturally a messy process. When I'm in the middle of a project or cooking dinner, my work space can look like a disaster area. My mother made valiant attempts to teach me to clean up as I go, but it never sank in and became a habit. I prefer to clean up after I'm finished. Better yet, I like to rely on the "I cook, you clean" agreement that my husband and I have so that he cleans. Now I recognize disorder as part of the chaordic continuum and turn to cleaning and organizing when I want to move away from chaos in the direction of order. Here are some tips that are useful in moving towards order:

Find an incentive for organizing:

- Jump on the spring cleaning bandwagon. Aim to finish major cleaning and repairs in time to relax during the heat of the summer.

- Plan a party for a few weeks out, and spruce your space up in preparation.

- Set a date for a yard sale, or contribute to one already organized by a local charity or a group of neighbors.

Set aside regular time for clearing

First thing in the morning may work well if you have lots of energy in the morning and like to start off with a clean slate. If you perk up later in the day, you might be better suited to organizing at the end of the day. Friday afternoon, for example, is my appointed time to file papers that have accumulated in my printer tray over the course of the week. One of my clients and her co-workers schedule regular "purge parties." It's not the prettiest image, but it does the trick of getting everyone to weed out the papers and clutter that are bogging them down. One advantage of hiring cleaning help is that you are forced to straighten up so they can come in and efficiently do their job. When you tidy up on a periodic basis, the chaos doesn't become so overwhelming.

Enlist support

- From a professional organizer: I've worked with professional organizers to set up filing systems for my paper and computer documents and my email. I've learned techniques that I wouldn't have thought of on my own, including color-coding my file folders, labeling the shelves of my linen closet so the white double bed sheets don't get mixed up with the white queen-sized sheets, and how to quickly clear a closet by sorting items into boxes labeled "trash," "recycle," "belongs somewhere else," "donate," "repair," and "undecided."

- From a buddy or family member: You can often increase your productivity and enjoyment by working in tandem, especially if you choose a partner who will keep you focused. Sometimes, like a virus, the organizing bug is easily spread to family members or roommates. Other times you may have to cajole others to pitch in. You can point out that since you aren't the only one making the mess, you shouldn't be the only one cleaning it up. Another strategy is to trade off with a friend, for example, weeding out her basement or closet one weekend and tackling yours the next.

- From a group: A group of coaching colleagues and I occasionally participate in something coaching pioneer, Thomas J. Leonard, called "Integrity Days." We all call into a telephone bridge line (a phone line for conference calls which accommodates multiple callers). In the first call, everyone shares what they want to accomplish. Then we hang up and get to work. We call in at the top of the next three or four hours to briefly report on our progress. It's amazing how much people complete with the support and accountability of a group!

May you, too, find "chaord" a freeing concept and find joy wherever you are in the balance between chaos and order.

~~~~~~

Resources:

www.napo.net—You can find a professional organizer in your area from this site of the National Association for Professional Organizers.

www.freecycling.org—Based on the premise that one man's trash is another's treasure, this national organization links people who want to get rid of things to people who want them.

www.flylady.net—This site offers lots of effective and humorous organizing tips and structures. I had to chuckle at the definition of CHAOS (Can't Have Anyone Over Syndrome).
~~~~~~

Overbooked: Hard Lessons Learned

Have you ever been late because you didn't budget time for the unexpected? Have you ever tried to squeeze so much in that you lost sight of what was most important? Have you ever made assumptions only to be proven wrong? Well, I confess, I've been found guilty on all counts and have sometimes paid dearly for it. Here's one such story that I'll share in hopes that you, as well, may learn from my lessons.

Some years ago, in mid-April, my family and I were scheduled to fly to Florida for a long anticipated vacation. I'd booked our trip the previous summer, bought new bathing suits and sunscreen, packed the weekend before, arranged for a neighbor to bring in the mail and care for our cat, confirmed our flights, and given our itinerary to our families and Florida hosts. Despite our best-laid plans, we made a few critical errors, which as I'll explain, made us miss our flight and could have jeopardized our entire vacation.

Here's what I learned from our experience:

First lesson: stay focused on your top priority
My husband, Bill, was coaching my youngest son's soccer team at the time. The very first game of the season was the morning of our trip. Since their team had an early start time and we'd miss the second game because of vacation, I encouraged them to go. We figured if they left right after their game, there would still be time to shower and change before leaving for the airport.

My older son and I stayed behind, and I bustled around, packing a few last minute items, cleaning the refrigerator, and vacuuming. Since we wouldn't have a meal or snack on the plane, I even prepared a quick meal to eat before we left. None of these activities were particularly critical, but I figured since we had time before our flight, I'd do what I could to make our return easier.

Second lesson: give yourself ample reserves of time
The first leg of our flight was scheduled for noon. I wanted to allow plenty of time to check-in and go through security. I didn't want so much time that we'd have to hang around the airport for hours, particularly because we had a long layover before the second leg of our journey. I went to the airport's website and found that they recommended allowing two hours for peak

travel times (5:00-7:00 a.m. and 2:30-6:00 p.m.) and an hour otherwise. In determining when to leave, we allotted a little more than an hour at the airport, gave ourselves twenty minutes to park, and figured travel time to the airport would be fifty minutes with some traffic. What we didn't factor in were any mishaps ... and we had one. Fifteen minutes into the trip to the airport, Bill remembered that he hadn't put one son's bag in the car—it was still on his bed!

Third lesson: don't assume

In weighing whether or not we had time to go back for my son's bag, I recalled a recent scene at the airport. A month earlier, at the same airport, I heard ticket agents chastise a passenger who was rushing to check in a half hour before his flight. The ticket agent explained that within thirty minutes of a scheduled departure, there was no guarantee of getting him and/or his luggage on the flight. After sharing this story, we figured that even if we doubled back, we'd still be able to check in well before the half hour cut-off mark. Hoping we'd make it, we rushed home to retrieve the bag and made it to the airport with fifty minutes to spare. Bill dropped me off with the boys and the bags to begin checking in while he parked the car. I was happy to see no check-in lines, but my hopes were quickly dashed when the ticket agent told us the flight was overbooked, and they'd already given our seats away. Despite my protests, they told me the best they could do was have us fly standby (slim prospects for a family of four, especially with other standby passengers ahead of us) or rebook us on a flight the next day.

Fortunately, we were able to fly out the following morning at 6:00 a.m. We took a different approach for that flight. We left all the bags in the car overnight, allowed plenty of travel time, even though there were no cars on the road, and arrived at the airport at 4:15 a.m. All in all, we had a marvelous vacation. Every day was sunny and above eighty degrees. Our hosts thoroughly spoiled us with lovely meals on their lanai and overnight babysitting. We swam in the Gulf no more than twenty feet from a pair of frolicking dolphins and spied six alligators and fifty turtles during a boat ride down the Braden river. We also discovered a new culinary treat—fried alligator—which my sometimes finicky son swore, "tastes just like chicken!" And we certainly learned some valuable lessons along the way.

Growing Season

I'm an avid gardener, and in doing some research about optimum planting times, I stumbled upon information about gardening by the moon. Although it's new to me, people have been planting by the moon for thousands of years. The trusted *Farmer's Almanac* makes planting and harvesting recommendations based upon the lunar cycle. It's opened up new avenues of learning for me in the areas of gardening, honoring natural rhythms, and astrology. Never an avid science student, I now find myself eagerly conducting experiments in the field. I can't wait to see if the broccoli I plant according to the optimal moon phase and astrological sign produces more than the control group of plants that I planted at the "wrong time." I'm having such fun doing something in a new way. As a result, my plants aren't the only thing growing—I am as well.

I work with many clients who are doing new things. It's a privilege to witness their learning and growth. They often stretch beyond their comfort zone to embark on new careers, launch new businesses, discover new ways to market, break out of limiting beliefs, and create new habits. It's always easiest to stick with the status quo—with what's known and comfortable. But if you keep doing things the same way, you'll keep getting the same results. So much more is possible when you open yourself up to new approaches.

Fear holds many people back from attempting something new. While fear can serve a useful function—warning you of danger—it can also keep you immobilized. To find out if fear is helping or holding you back, here's a technique I learned from master coach and author, Cheryl Richardson. Examine your fear to see if it's mixed with excitement or dread. If it's coupled with excitement that's equivalent to a green light. Dread indicates a red light. For example, even though I've had ample practice and am an accomplished public speaker, I often feel anxious before giving a speech or presentation. When I look into my fear, I see an eagerness to connect with my audience. I have a desire to see their eyes light up with new understanding, and I want to feel that I've done a good job communicating my message. I don't wish I could fast forward past the experience or regret accepting the invitation to speak.

If you got the thumb's up but still find yourself holding back, these steps can help you find the courage to proceed:

Ask yourself:
- o What's the worst that could happen?
- o Could you withstand the most negative consequences?
- o How would you be able to pick yourself back up?
- o What might you learn from this experience?

Then look at the flip side.
- o What is the very best possible outcome?
- o In your wildest dreams, what could come from this?
- o How would this make a difference in your life?
- o How might you grow from this experience?

Often there is a wide range of possibilities along the spectrum from catastrophic to copasetic. Once they confront their fears, most people realize that they'd be able to survive even the very worst case scenario. They also can easily identify measures to take to mitigate risks and to pave the way for success.

So whether you are learning a new skill at work, experimenting with a new technique in a hobby, discovering a different region of the world, or trying a new recipe, don't let fear stop you from growing.

~~~~~~

Resources:

www.gardeningbythemoon.com—On this site you'll find information about gardening by the moon and calendars for purchase.

Stand Up for Your Life: A Practical Step-by-Step Plan to Build Inner Confidence and Personal Power, by Cheryl Richardson

Feel the Fear and Do It Anyway, by Susan Jeffers

Taming Your Gremlin: A Surprisingly Simple Method for Getting Out of Your Own Way, by Richard Carson

www.toastmasters.org—This international organization has helped hundreds of thousands of people improve their communication skills and overcome fears of public speaking.
~~~~~~

When Duty Calls

In the spring of 2007, for the first time in my life, I had jury duty. Previously, when I've been summoned as a standby juror, I've never had to report. I hoped this trend would continue because I longed to have an unscheduled day that I could devote to writing. However, when I called the courthouse to check on the standby status, I heard, "All jurors need to report at 8:00 a.m." So I set an early alarm, printed directions, packed a lunch, and gathered my writing supplies (just in case there would be some time to work), in preparation to serve my civic duty.

This made me think about other obligations and how we handle them. We are born into some obligations. I know I often say, "We all need to do our part in this family," as I remind my kids of their chores. Other situations that create obligations, such as getting married and having children, we step into eagerly, anticipating that the rewards will far outweigh the costs. Sometimes we see a need and step in to make a difference with gifts of time or money. Then there are responsibilities associated with the rights we enjoy, such as paying taxes, exercising our right to vote, and serving on a jury.

Sometimes we feel conflicted about obligations. Those in the "sandwich generation" who care for children as well as aging or ailing parents may be especially familiar with this pull. Here's a process that can help in deciding how to handle obligations:

1. Determine what's needed and what your role will be
Sometimes we assume that we are the only one who can do something, but that's not always the case. There may be a better person for the job or a different solution than what appears to be an obvious course of action. Consider:

- What would take care of the situation?
- What are the available options?
- What would allow for the highest good of all concerned?
- Who is best suited for what duties?

In the case of my jury duty, since I'd already had to reschedule the date, I knew I had no choice other than to report.

2. Show up
Follow through on your commitments. There's a stiff fine for shirking jury duty. Back when our country had a draft, draft-dodging was a criminal offense. Other situations may not have such serious repercussions, but you'll still face anger or disappointment from those you let down. You'll also need to be able to live with yourself and the choice you made.

When I arrived at the courthouse, I went through a security checkpoint and joined the other potential jurors in a small, crowded room in the basement of the courthouse.

3. Make the best of it
Even if it's a duty that you take on begrudgingly, it could end up being a positive experience. Many people, for instance, have met their future spouses during training or service for the armed forces. (My mom and dad met at a Marine officers' training class at Quantico, VA.) I've also heard from those who've cared for the dying that it was one of their most rewarding experiences.

My fellow prospective jurors and I were told that the hardest part about jury duty would be the waiting. Many cases settle, but we would need to stay until they determined if any of the day's cases would go to trial. After watching a video which explained the process, we were sent on a forty-five minute break. It was a lovely day, and I found a sunny bench in a small park near the courtyard where I wrote until it was time to return. Once we got back, we had a very long wait. During this time, I edited several pieces which I planned to include in this book, revised the introduction, and began writing a newsletter. I had a very productive morning! At 12:30 p.m. the judge dismissed us and thanked us for doing our part to support the judicial system. Even though we weren't impaneled, this counted as jury duty, so we won't be summoned for another three years.

I'd already made the most of the day by getting more done than I would have otherwise, but it got even better. The courthouse was in Lynn, a seaside town and was only a few miles from the beach. With my bagged lunch and the beach chair and sun hat that I always keep in my car trunk for sports games, I enjoyed a perfect picnic on the beach. I wrote a bit more and then took a long walk on the beach before heading home. Sometimes duties have unexpected blessings.

Moving Conversations

Have you ever had a great conversation that buoyed you up for the whole day? That's how I felt once after talking with a limo driver on the way to the airport for a business trip. It made me wonder what it would be like if uplifting conversations like this were the norm, instead of the exception. We all are active partners in numerous conversations everyday. Let's see what lessons we can learn from the limo driver to turn more of these into empowering conversations. Imagine the possibilities!

Start the conversation
I don't remember exactly how our conversation started. It was probably a simple, straightforward question related to my trip, such as, "Where are you headed?" A good conversationalist doesn't need to be concerned about having a perfect opening line. Being focused on others and genuinely interested in what they have to say is what opens the door to engaging dialogue.

Ask questions
The limo driver was curious about my work. He'd heard of coaching and asked me a number of questions about how I got into the field, what people work on with coaches, and how coaching makes a difference.

Be willing to share
No one likes to be peppered with questions. The limo driver instinctively knew how to move back and forth between asking questions, making observations, and sharing his knowledge, experiences, and opinions.

Build rapport
At one point I hesitated slightly before telling him about the two books I'm writing. I wasn't sure what he'd make of my book topics and working titles, *Balance with Grace: Celebrate the Kaleidoscope of Life* and *Coffee Table Spirit*. Since he'd already been so open and supportive, however, I decided to risk it.

Respect different perspectives
The conversation became even livelier after I mentioned my writing. He had a keen interest in work/life balance and some interesting perspectives on spirituality. Our religious orientations were slightly different, but he respected my opinions even when they differed from his.

Be supportive, not critical
You may think that you are doing someone a favor by pointing out potential pitfalls with their project, but this is like poking holes in their dreams. Most of us have enough trouble quieting the voices of our own inner critics. Don't add yours to the chorus. If the limo driver had any doubts about the merits of my work, he thankfully kept them to himself. In fact, our conversation made me even more focused and confident that my books' messages were valuable and timely.

"Never give advice unless asked."—German proverb
My limo driver didn't offer any advice, only encouragement, which was just what I wanted. Even when it's given with the best of intentions, unsolicited advice delivers an underlying message that the recipient isn't doing things right or isn't capable of independently finding a solution. I know it's hard to refrain from passing along tips and suggestions, especially if you are a "helper" type like me. To be on the safe side, get permission before sharing. You could ask, "May I offer a suggestion/alternative for you to consider?" Don't take it personally if someone declines or chooses not to follow your advice. Everyone must find his or her own way.

Have fun experimenting with these suggestions in your conversations to see what results. Maybe, like the limo driver, you'll give someone just the boost they need to move forward with their life's dream.

~~~~~~

Resources:

Crucial Conversations, by Kerry Patterson, Joseph Grenny, Ron McMillan, and Al Switzler

How to Talk So Kids Will Listen and Listen So Kids Will Talk, by Adele Faber and Elaine Mazlish
~~~~~~

Unexpected Treasures

Memorial Day weekend is always fun, but one year's holiday particularly stands out because it was full of unexpected treasures.

First of all, it was a gift that school administrators chose a Friday before a long weekend for a curriculum day. While teachers and administrators use curriculum days for planning and training, these are welcome days off for students. In our town, they usually schedule these days in the middle of the week. To have a curriculum day tacked onto an already long weekend was a rare treat. We were already planning to spend the weekend with extended family at a shared beach cottage, and we relished this bonus day.

Next, after weeks of cool temperatures and dismal weather, and despite forecasts for more of the same, we were surprised by a sunny, warm weekend. Memorial Day weekend has always been the unofficial kickoff of summer, the date by which you can safely plant geraniums and wear white shoes. It was lovely to have the weather cooperate. We spent hours on the beach, without sweatshirts. A few brave souls, namely my husband and older son, briefly ventured into the chilly waters. After the weekend we reverted back into a dreary weather pattern. Memories of that sparkling weekend, however, reminded me to savor the days, both for the rains that soaked the gardens and the sun that occasionally peeked out from behind clouds.

Finally, during a walk on the beach with my nieces and sons, I found, not one, but two pieces of cobalt blue sea glass! Years ago, my mother-in-law introduced me to collecting sea glass. I've been combing beaches ever since, searching for jewel-like pieces washed up by the latest tide. In case you're not familiar with sea glass, they are pieces of broken glass that the sea turns from trash into treasure. Over time, waves and sand smooth jagged edges and buff once-shiny surfaces to a burnished matte finish. I've long been on the hunt for coveted blue pieces. Not only is blue my favorite color, but the small pieces of blue sea glass also remind me of sapphires, my favorite gemstone. Blue sea glass probably comes from old, broken Milk of Magnesia bottles. Blue pieces are understandably much rarer than green, white, or brown pieces, which come from soda, wine, and beer bottles. I've been with others when they've found blue pieces and have had false hopes on many occasions when I thought a broken mussel shell was one. Now, at long last, I have blue pieces to add to my collection. My prized blue pieces now top off a glass bowl filled with sea glass that I use as a dining table centerpiece. Every time I see them, I'm reminded of the of rush excitement in finding my first blue piece and then, not even thirty yards from that, another blue bit!

I think that our lives are filled with more gems than we realize, but unfortunately we often either pass right by them without notice or we take them for granted.

- What are the unexpected treasures surfacing in your life?
- How have you recently been pleasantly surprised?
- What instances of serendipity have you encountered?
- What wish has been granted?

This summer, I challenge you to be more aware of and more grateful for all the riches and gifts that bless your life. Happy treasure hunting!

No Worries

I love the popular phrase "no worries" that's often used as a response to someone's thanks, in lieu of "you're welcome," "no problem," or "not at all." I like the lightness and wisdom it simultaneously imparts. I only wish it were as easy to adopt as a mindset!

I am a Reiki student and often repeat the following Reiki principles as a morning meditation:

Just for today
Do not be angry
Do not worry
Be grateful
Work hard
Be kind to others

Most of these principles are "no problem" for me, but the one I occasionally wrestle with is the third one: "Do not worry." I find that worry comes in all shape and sizes, ranging from "Will it ever stop raining?" to "When will the economy rebound?" and "How will the latest round of budget cuts impact my children's education?" As I imagine I'm not alone in this struggle, I'll offer some of the steps I've found to help keep worry at bay.

Attention: what do you notice?
The first step is awareness. Pay attention to the physical clues that indicate you are worrying. Do you frown and wrinkle your brow? Does your stomach feel like it's in knots? Do your shoulders and neck tighten up? Do you pick or bite your nails, bounce your leg, or have other nervous habits that reflect your inner angst? Examine what messages these physical symptoms may hold for you. Knots and tension, for instance, may be your body's way of telling you to loosen up. A sinking feeling in the pit of your stomach may be a warning sign that you are about to make an unwise move. The earlier you catch yourself beginning to worry, the easier it is to turn worry into something more productive.

Whoa: don't go there!
Napoleon Hill in his classic *Think and Grow Rich* was one of the first to write about how thoughts create reality. When we play out the worst case scenario in our mind and dwell on it, it often becomes a self-fulfilling prophecy. My years of playing tennis have convinced me of this. When serving for a critical point, if I

allow the horrible thought of double faulting to enter and stay in my mind, I usually do. It's important to turn negative thoughts around as soon as possible before they can wreak havoc.

About face: choose a different perspective
Visualization can help you switch direction, away from worry, into confident action or peaceful acceptance. Play a different mental tape, replacing the worst case scenario with the least successful outcome that would still satisfy you. Then let your imagination go as you picture an amazingly happy ending in your mind's eye. Freeze frame here! If you keep this as your vision, you'll automatically start figuring out how to make it happen and new possibilities will open up for you.

If you're not sure whether action or acceptance would be best in your situation, this excerpt from the "Serenity Prayer" by Reinhold Niebuhr may help you decide:

God grant me the serenity to accept the things
I cannot change;
Courage to change the things I can;
And wisdom to know the difference.

Onward and upward: trust as you go
Leave worry behind you as you move on, by either taking action or detaching from the situation. Sometimes the situation will unfold exactly as you'd dreamed. Every so often things won't work out the way you'd hoped. Although it isn't always easy, it's important to trust that things will eventually work out in the best way. Sometimes what's next or best for us is something we don't expect at all.

For example, there was a time in my twenties when I felt as if all my dreams were unraveling. I had just moved to Boston to marry my college sweetheart when, less than two months from walking down the aisle, I learned some things that made me call off the wedding. It was one of the lowest points of my life. At the time, I couldn't see how anything positive could possibly come from it. Looking back, I'm so grateful things turned out as they did. It was at my new workplace that I met Bill, whom I've been incredibly happily married to since 1990!

If over time you've earned the nickname of "worrywart," you may not be able to conquer the worry habit overnight. With attention and practice, however, I'm sure you'll surmount many of life's worries. Are you ready to accept the challenge? Here's to many carefree days this summer ... with "No worries!"

~~~~~~

Resources:

Think and Grow Rich, by Napoleon Hill

The Inner Game of Tennis: The Mental Side of Peak Performance, by Timothy Gallwey
~~~~~~

Joyful Abandon

My younger son has the most delightful habit of skipping. Often in the parking lot of our health club, he'll take a few steps, add a little bounce, and he's off—skipping all the way to the door. One winter while my older son was in karate class, he and I would often spend time in the gym. I'd walk around the inside track while he played basketball. Sometimes he'd take a break from shooting hoops to walk with me. The walk would turn into a skip, and then I'd join him in skipping a lap or two. What fun! The moments of being airborne felt like flying, and it was impossible not to smile and laugh.

This summer I'm looking for more ways to bring that same feeling of joyful abandon into our lives. During a family brainstorming session we came up with the following ideas:

- go fishing
- climb Mt. Lincoln (Our goal is to hike all of the Presidential Mountains in NH.)
- make cookies
- go to a Japanese steakhouse
- play tennis
- hold ping-pong tournaments
- make sandcastles and do yoga on the beach
- go to a water park
- read the latest Harry Potter book
- go sailing
- go to the movies
- add to our sea glass collection
- pick berries
- go to a museum or planetarium
- take a picnic to an outdoor concert

Even if you don't have young children, there are many ways you can play like a child this summer. To find them, ask yourself:

- What is your heart calling you to do?
- What's your body yearning to do?

- o How could you lose yourself for a few hours?
- o What would make time feel like it was standing still?

Make your own summer fun list, and jump right in! Or, as the line from the childhood game, Hokey Pokey, instructs: "Put your whole self in and shake it all about ... That's what it's all about!"

~~~~~~

Resources:

The Kids' Summer Handbook, by Jane Drake and Ann Love

Sandtiquity: Architectural Marvels You Can Build at the Beach, by Malcolm Wells, Kappy Wells, and Sonnie Simo

Pillsbury Best Cookies Cookbook: Favorite Recipes from America's Most-Trusted Kitchens, by the Pillsbury Company

www.pickyourown.org This site lists pick-your-own fruit and vegetable farms in the U.S.
~~~~~~

In Your Element

One year before school ended for the summer, I had an opportunity to chaperone a fifth grade field trip to explore tidal pools at Place Cove in Hampton, NH. It was my younger son's last year in elementary school, and I suspected that this might be my last invitation to join a field trip. I juggled my schedule to clear time for the excursion. Boy, was it worth it!

What fun we had during our time at the beach! We gingerly made our way along the rocks at the water's edge, occasionally slipping on patches of seaweed. The kids were fascinated by their exploration of the tidal pools. They frequently called out in excitement for others to come and view their discoveries. We found and handled starfish, sea urchins, sponges, crabs, shrimp, limpets, snails, mussels, and barnacles. After eating picnic lunches and drawing and writing in their science notebooks, the children and their teachers piled back onto the school buses for their return trip to school. The other parents immediately packed up to head home, but I couldn't bring myself to leave the beach right away.

It felt like the ocean was a magnet, drawing me into its field. Knowing I had plenty of time before I needed to be back in my office, I gave into its pull. I slipped off my shoes and set out for a walk on the beach, enjoying the give of the sand underfoot. In contrast to the hard pavement I usually walk on, I loved the way my feet sank into the sand with every stride. The sun, which had been a stranger over the last weeks, came out and welcomingly warmed my back as I walked along the water's edge. I let a few waves roll over my feet and was surprised that the water wasn't as bracing as I expected it to be so early in the season. The breeze off of the water cooled my face and brought with it the unmistakable briny, slightly fishy smell of the ocean. Other than a handful of walkers and sunbathers, the beach was deserted. The only sounds were those of lapping waves and screeching gulls. As I took in the sights of diving seabirds and picked up an interesting rock to add to my collection, I said to myself, "I'm in my element."

This mid-week break at the beach left me totally relaxed and rejuvenated, much the way a vacation or retreat would. It made me realize how important it is to create opportunities to connect to the natural world, especially to the elements or combinations of elements that most resonate with us. Whether it's a day at the beach, in the mountains, or in the garden, I hope you find plenty of opportunities this summer to be in your element. The following "Back to Nature" reading offers numerous suggestions for connecting with the elements.

Back to Nature

Every summer my family and I go camping in the White Mountains of NH. Our trip never fails to deliver everything a good vacation should: a complete escape from our everyday life, fun, adventure, and lots of good memories. During the days we do a lot of hiking. One of my favorite hikes was a six-hour trek to the 5,260-feet summit of Mt. Lafayette. We hiked across a ridge with breathtaking views of the Presidential Mountain range on either side, to the summit of Mt. Lincoln, and then down the Falling Waters trail, aptly named for its beautiful waterfalls. During our stay we cook all our meals over the campfire or propane stove, bathe in the brisk waters of the mountain stream bordering our campsite, and sleep in sleeping bags in tents. It's so peaceful listening to the crackle of the campfire, the bird calls, and the babbling brook. There's much that we gain from our time in the wild: resilience, resourcefulness, and the opportunity to reconnect with ourselves, each other, and the forest around us.

Although I realize that camping is not everyone's idea of a vacation, I think that many blessings can be derived from inviting nature to play a larger role in our lives. The outdoors is always there, beckoning us to relax, gain perspective, and return to center. Answer its call in your own favorite way or choose several of the following opportunities to connect with the elements:

Earth

- Go barefoot. Plant your feet firmly on the ground, and imagine roots growing out of the bottom of your feet, connecting you to the earth and firmly holding you in place.
- Explore local gardens, trails, and parks. In my town we are blessed with an abundance of state forest trails and a lovingly maintained property of The Trustees of Reservations.
- Eat meals outdoors—on your deck, patio, porch, front step, picnic blanket, or park bench.
- Work the soil. Plant flowers, vegetables, or herbs to harvest the earth's bounty. Weeding can be very therapeutic. I remember feeling compelled to weed the afternoon of September 11, 2001 and feeling more grounded afterwards.

Water

- Go to a beach, pond, or lake. Splash in the water. Float on your back, and feel yourself buoyed up.
- Go canoeing, kayaking, white-water rafting, or sailing.
- Go fishing. As most fishing hobbyists will tell you, it's not

about the fish. There's tranquility in silently watching and waiting.

- Watch the ripples in the water after throwing or skipping stones.

Fire

- Enjoy a campfire and all that accompanies it: S'mores, popcorn, ghost stories, songs (we make up silly verses about the day's adventures), and simply staring into the flames.
- Count fireflies.
- Light citronella or tiki torches to bring fire to your backyard and keep the mosquitoes away.
- Enjoy a fireworks display.
- Soak up the warmth and vitamin D from the sun.

Air

- Admire and look for species that take wing: birds, butterflies, dragonflies and bats.
- Go on a hot air balloon or glider ride, go parasailing, or take hang gliding lessons. We have some amazing memories and video footage from another family adventure at the hang gliding school at Jockey's Ridge State Park.
- Lie on the ground and watch the clouds. What pictures do they make?
- Catch some air. My most memorable camping adventure was jumping off a forty-foot cliff into an icy pool of water, proving to myself, and my stunned family, that I'd overcome a fear of heights. Less extreme choices might include jumping rope, going off the diving board, or jumping on a trampoline.

During the summer take full advantage of opportunities to reap the benefits of getting back to nature.

~~~~~~

Resources:

The Garden Primer, by Barbara Damrosch

The Kids' Campfire Book: Official Book of Campfire Fun, by Jane Drake, Ann Love, and Heather Collins

www.thetrustees.org—This site can help you discover some of the most scenic and historic properties in Massachusetts.
~~~~~~

A Reason to Celebrate

This time of year is marked by many celebrations of achievement and completion. There are end-of-school report cards, graduations, anniversaries, and here in the United States, the 4th of July.

How do you recognize achievements? Do you do anything special to mark reaching major milestones? Do you jump up and down shouting, "Woo Hoo!" or "Yippee"? Do you throw a party, or do you quietly press on without missing a beat? I've noticed in the marketing programs I lead that many people are resistant to selecting a reward for meeting a business goal. I've also witnessed how difficult it is for clients and teleclass participants to toot their own horns. If you're the type who tends not to celebrate your own accomplishments, here are some approaches that may change that.

Set the stage for success
With a big goal in mind, write a letter to your best friend, a family member, or someone else who has always been interested and supportive of your endeavors. Date this letter one to two years from now. Fast-forward and write from that vantage point, as if you are looking backwards on your successful completion of the goal. Explain why the goal was so important to you and how it feels to have finally achieved it. Describe how you and your life have changed as a result. Detail the steps you took and the milestones you attained along the way. Harness the power of your imagination to fill in the gaps of how you got from here to there easily, profitably, or serendipitously. It's your story, so invent the scenario that's most pleasing to you. Reread your letter frequently to remind yourself of your vision and to cement the belief that you really can achieve your goal. Let it spark the kindling of ideas to keep the fire of inspired action burning.

Variations: As an alternative to writing, record yourself having an imaginary conversation describing your steps to success, or use visualization to picture yourself attaining your goal.

Keep a success log
Many people make lists of things they have to do. To-do lists are fine time management tools, but they can become disheartening. There are always things left undone, and new items crop up all the time. To balance this out, keep another list—a success log—of all the things you have done. (Refer to "Stay Positive" in "First Steps" for more on success logs.) Record the smaller, more

mundane actions that slowly add up over time. Highlight your big accomplishments and "WOW" wins. When you are going for a big goal, it can feel discouraging when there are so many steps between you and your desired end point. If doubt or frustration sets in, pull out your success log to remind yourself of the progress you have made. Let it bring to mind the capabilities you possess that have contributed to your success to date. Update your success log frequently to celebrate and acknowledge new triumphs.

Reward yourself with a celebration
Celebrations give us opportunities to bask in the glory of our accomplishments. Often there's a big push at the end as we launch a new product, study for exams, or bring a project to completion by a certain deadline. This kind of pace and intensity can't be maintained for too long. Taking a vacation, spending a weekend away, or going out to dinner serve the dual purpose of rewarding and recharging us. In addition to being reminders to take pride in our achievements, celebratory occasions often let us reconnect with the people whom we may not have been able to spend as much time with during crunch periods. They give us a chance to let people know what we've been up to. In sharing news of our successes, we can be an inspiration to others. Our achievement may serve as a catalyst, spurring someone else to action. The win could be just the encouragement someone else needs to persevere and bring a project to completion. This can lead to even more reasons to celebrate.

Slowing Down into Summer

Are you living in the fast lane? Do you frequently find yourself multi-tasking, doing at least two different things at once? Do you rush from one activity to the next, driven by your day-planner, deadlines, and to-do lists? If this description fits you, you certainly have a lot of company. With modern technology, our society has become increasingly fast-paced. The Internet, email, voice mail, cellular phones, and smart phones, while convenient, have blurred the boundaries between work time and down time.

When is enough, enough? Through personal experience and my work with clients, I've learned that it may be time to slow down when:

- you feel overwhelmed
- you easily lose your patience
- you worry about how you'll get everything done
- you're stressed
- you find yourself in the wrong place at the wrong time
- you frequently get sick
- you're tired
- you forget things

If any of these resonated with you, consider taking a break and slowing your pace. Summer's the perfect time to slip into a slower gear. With rising temperatures and humidity, our bodies seem to crave leisure. Here are some ideas to help you slow down:

Figure out why you are so busy
Were you raised to have a strong work ethic? Do you feel guilty if you aren't doing something productive? How do you benefit by being so busy? Some people have such a strong need to accomplish or to be recognized for their efforts that their sense of self-worth is tied to what they do instead of to who they are. Recognizing that need and its origin is the first step to establishing a slower, more comfortable rhythm. To counteract busyness, practice doing nothing for a short period every day. If it's tempting to slip back into warp speed, remind yourself that you are a human *being*, not a human *doing*.

Declare a day of rest
Regardless of your religious background, instituting a Sabbath, or day of rest, can be a welcome respite after a busy week. Discover what activities you'd like to ban during your rest day. Laundry

and errands would top my list. Consider what activities you'd like to include, such as reading and a family dinner. Observing a rest day is one way to clearly delineate the boundaries between work and personal time.

Reduce your caffeine intake

Caffeine gives you the same type of rush as the adrenaline your body produces when you're in fight-or-flight situations. If you have a demanding schedule, caffeine will only exacerbate your stress. Cutting out or reducing coffee, tea, chocolate, and cola has a calming effect in addition to other healthful benefits. To avoid withdrawal headaches, reduce caffeine consumption gradually instead of going "cold turkey." This is most easily accomplished over the course of a week or two, by substituting an increasing amount of decaf for your regular coffee until you are drinking all or mostly decaf.

Reduce your sugar intake

Sugar can create the same buzz as caffeine, so eliminate or reduce it if you're seeking serenity. It's a tough one, but my clients who have accepted the "no sugar" challenge report that they have more energy and feel better without it.

Reduce your driving speed

This time of year, it's almost inevitable that a construction vehicle, camper, or other slow-moving vehicle will be in front of you for part of your journey. Allow extra time to get places so you won't rush and so that unexpected delays won't provoke road rage. At more moderate speeds, you won't have to worry about getting speeding tickets, you'll notice more things along the way, and you'll get better gas mileage.

Resist the temptation to do "just one more thing"

There will always be things to do. Prioritize, so you do what's most important to you. Be realistic about how much you and other family members can sanely accomplish in a given day. Instead of cramming more into an already tight schedule, look for opportunities to create some breathing room.

Take a deep breath

You have to breathe anyway, so why not make it a deep, belly breath? There are many different breathing techniques. Use this one the next time you feel harried: inhale slowly, filling your diaphragm and your lungs, breathing in peace. Briefly hold your breath. Then, slowly exhale, contracting your abdomen, releasing tension along with your breath. When the world feels like it's spinning out of control around you, focusing on your breathing will help you stay centered.

Be fully present

Catch yourself if you begin worrying about what's next on the agenda or if you start rehashing a past event. Gently return your focus to the here and now. After all, the present is where living takes place. The quality of your work will improve when you take your time and concentrate fully on the task at hand. Likewise, the quality of your relationships will improve if you give your full attention to others.

Say no

Even fun social engagements can become too much at times. Listen to your heart, and gracefully decline an invitation if it feels more like an obligation than a joy. If it's something you'd love to do but suspect it may be too much, in addition to your other commitments, leave it open if possible. It's better to underpromise by saying you'll try make it than to disappoint by canceling at the last minute.

Get away from it all

Everyone can benefit from a break in routine. Spending time away from work, with family, friends, or in solitude can give you a fresh perspective. Use this perspective to guide you in the choices you make upon your return. Whether your summer finds you at the shore, in the mountains, or in your own backyard, relax and enjoy the lazy days of summer!

~~~~~~~~~~~~~~~~~~~~~~~~~~~~~~~~~~~~~~~

Resources:

Adrenaline and Stress: The Exciting New Breakthrough that Helps You Overcome Stress Damage, by Archibald Hart

The Art of Being: Recapturing the Self, by Catherine Laroze
~~~~~~~~~~~~~~~~~~~~~~~~~~~~~~~~~~~~~~~

The Power of Now: A Guide to Spiritual Enlightenment, by Eckhart Tolle

Practicing the Power of Now: Essential Teachings, Meditations, and Exercises from The Power of Now, by Eckhart Tolle

20 Minute Retreats: Revive Your Spirits in Just Minutes a Day with Simple, Self-Led Practices, by Rachel Harris

Mitten Strings for God: Reflections for Mothers in a Hurry, by Katrina Kenison.

Gone Fishing

During a walk on the beach, I once had the following exchange with a young man who was surfcasting:

Me: Are you catching anything?
Fisherman: Not yet, but I've only been here about an hour.
Me: Well, keep at it.
Fisherman: Oh, I'm having fun, regardless.
Me: That's what matters most!

This conversation made me think of how often we fish for things in our lives: a new job, a different career, more clients, a life partner, the right words, the perfect outfit, or a new location. The list could go on and on!

- What are you currently hoping to hook?
- How do you view fishing? Is it a means to an end? A necessary evil? A process? An adventure?
- What do you feel as you cast your line for the first time? Anticipation? Excitement? Hope? Nervousness?
- How do you feel when you reel in an empty line for the umpteenth time? Aggravated? Frustrated? Hopeful? Angry? Discouraged? Impatient? Patient? Determined?

Successful fishermen and women:

- accept that some of their catch will get away—and may even take their bait! They understand that fishing is a process that usually requires repeated attempts.
- find joy in the fishing itself
- prepare, so in case a big one strikes, it won't break the line
- increase the odds by consulting the tide charts and choosing tempting bait
- know that it's not just about the catch

I wish you all the best with your fishing, regardless of what you are hoping to catch. May you enjoy lots of hits and the perfect catch! And if nothing's biting, simply enjoy the sun, the sound of the waves, and the experience!

Summer Simplicity

Those of us who live in the Northeast, where summer is often short, learn to squeeze as much sun and fun out of the summer as possible. Here are some ideas for streamlining and simplifying things on the home front this summer so that you can spend more time outside enjoying summer activities and people you love:

Stock up on essentials
Life becomes more complicated when you run out of things. For items that usually last a few weeks, such as printer cartridges and toiletries, you may need just one extra to create a comfortable margin of safety. More quickly-depleted items such as toilet paper, bottled drinks, and energy bars may require larger back-up quantities. Consider buying these in bulk at a wholesaler a few times a year. Develop the habit of replenishing perishable or difficult-to-store necessities including milk, juice, or gasoline before you are down to the last drop. For instance, you could discipline yourself to stop by the nearest gas station to fill up your tank whenever you reach the quarter tank mark.

Systematize
Certain activities that you do over and over, such as grocery shopping, menu planning, and packing, lend themselves well to systematization. Rather than wrack your brain to think of everything you'll need every time you begin the process, create a master list for each activity. For instance, you could make a grocery checklist with your favorite items divided by aisle in the grocery store where you usually shop. (This also makes the task easier to pass on to someone else.) Meal planning and entertaining are easier with a list of your family's favorite meals and menus that work well for company, along with an ingredient list. Preparing for a day at the beach or a camping trip is simplified with a list of everything you'll need, especially if many of the items are stored together.

Cancel subscriptions
If magazines and newspapers pile up around your house without being read, cancel the subscriptions. Bookmark the websites of your favorite Internet news services and magazines. You'll keep up with current events while cutting back on clutter and recycling.

Think twice before purchasing
Adopt a less-is-more mentality when it comes to shopping. If you've already worked hard to reduce household clutter, you don't want unnecessary purchases to set you back in your efforts. Ask yourself before you buy whether the effort of taking care of the new purchase and finding a place to store it will simplify or complicate your life. Only buy what you truly love and need. Shop with a list, and refrain from impulse purchases. Rather than buying DVDs, books, audiotapes, computer games, and power tools, could you rent, borrow, or share instead?

Lighten up on the cooking
If it feels too hot to cook, don't. Enjoy cold suppers of sandwiches, salads, or fresh fruit when it's sweltering outside. Get creative with leftovers: use them as omelet fillings, in wrap sandwiches, or as a topping for pasta. Even during cool weather, think of ways to use "planned overs." That extra rice, pasta, or grilled meat can become the basis for the next night's meal, with a fraction of the preparation time.

Reduce laundry and dry-cleaning
Folding your laundry as soon as it comes out of the dryer practically eliminates the need for ironing. To cut down on laundry and make your clothes last longer, encourage family members not to put clothes into the hamper until they are dirty. Check labels before buying clothing, and when possible avoid buying clothes that need to be dry-cleaned. Experiment with wrinkle-reducing sprays and in-the-dryer dry-cleaning products now on the market.

Leave your shoes by the door
Floors and carpets stay cleaner if you remove your shoes when you come inside. In many countries this is the custom, and it's a sensible one. If you like the support of shoes, reserve a pair for indoor use only. In Germany, these are called *Hausschuhe*, or house shoes. To help young children do this independently, buy shoes with Velcro fasteners.

Experiment with these strategies, and look for additional ways to make things easier. You may discover what many from the Voluntary Simplicity movement already have: that a simple life is a good life.

~~~~~~

Resources:

Living the Simple Life: A Guide to Scaling Down and Enjoying More, by Elaine St. James

The Simple Living Guide, by Janet Luhrs

Living Simply: Choosing Less in a World of More, by Joanne Heim

Cook Once, Eat Twice Slow Cooker Recipes, by Better Homes and Gardens
~~~~~~

Pack Lightly

After spending a lot of time unpacking uneaten food and unworn clothing from a long holiday weekend away with my family, I realized I could benefit from packing more lightly. When I think about it, I'm also aware that my suitcase isn't the only thing I tend to overfill. In scheduling, I've often created overzealous agendas. There are definite corollaries between how I pack my suitcase and how I pack my schedule.

How do you pack? Do you cram items in so that your suitcase is full-to-bursting? Are you a minimalist, including only what's necessary and important? Or are you somewhere in the middle, adding enough but keeping room left over for interesting things that cross your path? In case you haven't guessed, my tendency is toward the fuller side. I'm always tempted to pack in "just one more thing." However, with summer travel and kids out of school, the simpler approach now seems more appealing. Here are some ways I've thought of to streamline:

Pare down to essentials

Summer is the perfect time to lighten our loads. In the literal sense, summer clothes are less bulky, so we don't have to be encumbered by heavy bags. Bathing suits and quick-drying fabrics make it easy to pack a few changes of clothes for a week's trip, plus toiletries, in a small suitcase. The long-awaited nice weather also makes us eager to whittle down our schedules, so we can spend less time working inside and more time playing outside. In the process of planning and packing it's helpful to ask:

- What do I really want?
- What's most important to include?
- What would feel like enough?
- What do I want to leave out?

Include flexible options

Mixing and matching is the key to a versatile wardrobe and an adjustable schedule. In areas such as my New England surroundings, where summer Fahrenheit temperatures can range from forty to ninety degrees, we keep comfortable with layered pieces that can be added or subtracted as it warms up or cools down. Although weather forecasts can help us decide what to pack for the weekend or what to wear for the day, predictions aren't always accurate. It's important to be flexible. Likewise, we can carefully plan out a day's schedule, but unexpected circumstances—a sick child or pet, a severe storm, a work crisis —may demand immediate attention, dictating a change in plans. When we have to revamp or make last minute changes, it's good to consider:

- What would serve me best?
- What could I do differently?
- What other choices do I have?
- What parts can I combine to make a pleasing whole?

Leave room for treasures

When we struggle to squeeze everything in, we run the risk of missing out on some rare finds. If you can barely zip your suitcase at the beginning of a trip, there will be no room to tuck in the perfect conch shell you find at the beach or the collectible you fancy at an antiques show. If your day is so tightly booked with commitments, you could easily miss the double rainbow on display outside your window. Leave room for the unexpected, for you may be pleasantly surprised. Beautiful things crop up around the edges, like the lone lady's slipper—an endangered wildflower—blooming at the edge of the woods that I've noticed on recent walks.

To and Fro

Vacations and long weekends provide fun, healthy breaks from work and the routine of everyday life. While planning and anticipation can add to the excitement of a vacation, sometimes there are so many things to take care of before going away that it makes you wonder if it's worth it. Other times the physical strain from travel or higher level of activity (such as the stiffness I feel after a long weekend of hiking and camping) makes it feel like you need a vacation to recover from your vacation. My clients sometimes ask for coaching around how to smoothly prepare for and return from vacations or time away from home. Although I'm still working on mastering these transitions, I'm happy to share some of the strategies I've found helpful:

Clear the decks
You will settle back in more easily if you tie up as many loose ends as possible before you depart. Do your best to catch up on bills, correspondence, laundry, chores, and the most pressing of your to-dos before you leave. Don't go overboard, though, or you'll spend the first couple days decompressing from the exhaustion and stress of your preparations.

Create systems
People who travel all the time are able to pack at a moment's notice. Their toiletry bags are stocked, and they've learned from experience what they need to bring and what they can do without. If you take the same type of trip every year, a checklist, as mentioned in "Summer Simplicity," is a great way to make sure you remember the essential gear.

Give yourself a break
Technology has made it easy to stay connected to work while physically away from your office. This doesn't mean it's a good idea. Arrange for a trusted colleague or virtual assistant to handle things in your absence, or use an automated "out of office" message to reply to emails and phone calls. Leave work totally behind, or limit your check-ins to give yourself a true vacation.

Leave things in good hands
Don't worry about your home, pets, mail, and plants while you are away. Trade with a neighbor, or pay a local teen or house/pet sitter to tend to things on the home front. Provide detailed instructions and emergency contact information so you can rest easy.

Schedule catch-up time
Leave plenty of open time in your schedule upon your return. Consider returning from a long trip on a Saturday to give you a full day to settle in before the work week. Ease into your first day back at work by blocking off at least the morning to prioritize and respond to your accumulated messages and requests.

Take advantage of a fresh perspective
Pay attention to what you missed while away, as this may give you a clue about what you'd like to make more of a priority. (On a recent trip for me, for instance, it was playing the piano.) Also notice what you dread returning to or suddenly can no longer tolerate. This may point to areas crying out for a change.

Hold on to that vacation feeling
Don't be in a rush to return to life as usual. If you tend to be more spontaneous while traveling, exploring new places, trying new foods, and talking to strangers, don't step out of the role of adventurer because you are home. Expand your awareness of the choices around you in your own community. Look for ways to make every day feel like a holiday.

Keeping the "Happy" in "Happy Anniversary"

Relationships require regular maintenance and, at times, hard work, to keep running smoothly. Good communication is the most essential element of this regular maintenance. The challenges of making ends meet, creating a home, and perhaps even raising a family, can bring a couple close together or can drive them apart. Here are some tips for enhancing communication and closeness between you and your significant other:

Communicate early
There is a wise old adage that says, "Never let the sun go down on your anger." So often we keep small irritations to ourselves, instead of bringing them out in the open. If we don't let go of these feelings but allow them to fester, they become bigger and are often blown out of proportion. It's better to quickly and lightly—with humor, if possible—bring something to your partner's attention before it becomes a big deal. Addressing things early is one way to foster discussions instead of fights.

Communicate constructively
No one enjoys being criticized or blamed. If that's your tack, don't be surprised if you get a defensive reaction. Instead of making the other person wrong or comparing them unfavorably to someone else, be unconditionally constructive in what you say. Point out the positives and make simple requests. Practice being direct with your language and saying what needs to be said without diminishing the other person.

Communicate fully
If you've been in a relationship for a long time, you may think that the two of you can read each other's minds. That's a dangerous assumption to make. You may not really know what the other is feeling, wanting, or needing unless you ask for clarification. So if you've had a hard day and could use a hug, ask for it. If your partner does something nice for you, acknowledge it. And if the urge to say, "I love you" strikes, go ahead and say it. So many disappointments and hurt feelings in relationships are caused by not speaking up and letting your partner know what's on your mind.

Communicate with compassion
Stephen Covey in his book *The 7 Habits of Highly Effective People* encourages his readers to seek first to understand, then to be understood. From our own point of view, we are always right, so

the other person must be wrong. Fully listening to your partner to get his or her take on a situation shows that you care and that you respect differing opinions. It's easier to arrive at a win-win compromise if you set the stage with understanding.

Communicate often

Given the average busy lifestyle, I often hear the complaint, "There isn't time to really connect with my spouse." Conversations between parents often revolve around honey-do's: "Honey, do you think you can do the grocery shopping/laundry/yard work today?" or scheduled activities: "I'll drop him off if you can pick him up." It's important to step away from the day-to-day details and devote some time to the two of you. Date nights, after dinner walks, and periodic romantic getaways are all great ways to open up the lines of communication and recapture the magic that first drew the two of you together.

Whether you are celebrating your first month of dating or your fiftieth year of marriage, good communication will help you keep the "happy" in "happy anniversary."

~~~~~~

Resources:

The Seven Habits of Highly Effective People, by Stephen Covey

The Four Agreements and *The Mastery of Love,* by Don Miguel Ruiz

Social Intelligence: The New Science of Human Relationships, by Daniel Goleman
~~~~~~

Powerful Forces

One summer, my family and I had a spectacular vacation in the Southwest. Our primary destination was "The Grand Staircase," which includes Bryce, Zion, and the North Rim of the Grand Canyon. Along the way we also visited Las Vegas, Red Rock Canyon, Valley of Fire, Coral Sand Dunes, and Lake Powell. On numerous hikes and drives we were awed by breathtaking scenery. We saw incredible formations: arches, buttes, mesas, sheer cliffs, spires, and hoodoos, which reminded me of sand dribbles I used to make with the now-vintage toy "Silly Sand." Some rocks looked like beehives, and one had markings that resembled a checkerboard.

What's most amazing is that, with the exception of Las Vegas, which is steeped in commercialism, all of the fanciful shapes and structures were shaped by Nature. It's a bit of an oversimplification of the geologic processes involved, but basically these wonders were formed by two powerful forces: uplift and erosion. Around seventeen million years ago, pressures within the Earth began to uplift and form what is known as the Colorado Plateau. In the highest spots this area was about three miles above sea level. Over time water, ice, and wind gradually eroded the land, carving out the canyons. The rivers—the Colorado in the Grand Canyon, the Sevier in Bryce, and the Virgin in Zion—continue to change the shape of the canyons.

If uplift and erosion are powerful enough to shape rock, image the impact these forces have on human life. Consider:

- What are the forces currently shaping the landscape of your life?
- What powerful forces do you choose to set into motion?
- How might your thoughts, words, and actions erode people and situations around you?
- What can you do to uplift yourself and others?

Rise to the challenge of being a positive force in the world and seek opportunities to uplift instead of erode.

Fall

Work that Works

In the U.S. we celebrate Labor Day on the first Monday of September. Spawned in 1882 by the labor movement, the holiday recognizes the contributions of the American worker. Although Labor Day is now marked less by labor rallies and speeches than end-of-summer cookouts and back-to-school sales, it's a good occasion to pause and reflect upon work and how it's working for you.

How does it feel to return to work, whether paid or unpaid, after time off? Do you enjoy your work and come back full of ideas and renewed energy? Do you wake up in a crabby mood every work day and wish you could call in sick? Do you watch the clock, counting down the hours to quitting time, or do you sometimes get so absorbed in your work that time flies by?

What do you think about work? I think that:

- we spend such a high percentage of our waking hours at work; we'd better enjoy what we do.
- work is only one part of a balanced life. It should serve you and your life instead of the other way around.
- who you are is not what you do. So many people get wrapped up in the trappings of their work (the title, the prestige, the professional image) that their sense of self-worth becomes tied to their job performance. In an economy where layoffs and salary freezes are commonplace, this can be debilitating.
- we all have a life purpose—something that we are meant to contribute. Each of us has been dealt a unique set of strengths, preferences, and personality characteristics with which to accomplish what Buddhists call our "right livelihood."
- when we discover and begin living our purpose, there can be an ease and flow to work that makes work feels like play.

So what do you do if your work isn't working for you? How do you go about finding out what would be both fulfilling and profitable? How can you redesign your work environment or your job description so you can't help but succeed? How do you go about making a career change if that's needed?

When I coach clients in these situations, the overarching process we use can be broken down into three basic steps: ***who***, ***what***, and ***how***. Spending time in the beginning clarifying ***who*** you are makes it easier to find ***what*** work is a good fit for you. Once you've determined your ideal work, the final piece is looking at ***how*** to move into it. Within this framework, some things to explore are:

Who: What are your values, your natural gifts, your skills, your personality characteristics, and learning styles? What motivates you, what are you passionate about, and what are your quirks? What difference do you make to others? What is your life purpose? There are many exercises, assessments, and lines of inquiry that can shed light on ***who*** is the sum total of all these elements.

What: Not all of your values will be expressed through work, and not all of your needs will be met through it. The awareness of what makes you tick and what makes you happy, however, makes it easier to determine ***what*** industry, occupation, scope of responsibility, and size of company would make a good fit for you.

How: Restructuring your job, job-sharing, moving to another job within the same company, going back to school, moonlighting, updating your resume, and launching a job search are all examples of ***how*** you can move into more fulfilling work.

If your work's not working, don't settle for feeling stuck and frustrated. Do something about it! One place to start is at your library or bookstore. Some of the books I use with and recommend to clients include:

Now What? Ninety Days to a New Life Direction, by Laura Berman Fortgang—I work with Laura and frequently use this powerful book and process to help clients discover their Life Blueprint.™

Finding Your North Star: Claiming the Life You Were Meant to Live, by Martha Beck

Soul Mission Life Vision: Recognize Your True Gifts and Make Your Mark in the World, by Alan Seale

Work with Passion: How to Do What You Love for a Living, by Nancy Anderson

Choice Points: Navigate your Career Using the Unique PaperRoom Process, by Sydney Rice

Callings: Finding and Following an Authentic Life, by Gregg Lavoy

A New Earth: Awakening to Your Life's Purpose, by Eckhart Tolle

Get Hired NOW! by C.J. Hayden and Frank Traditi

Career transitions can be confusing, frustrating, and at times, downright scary. It can help to team up with a coach or career counselor to help you discover what would make you "whistle while you work." They may not be able to teach you how to whistle, (For years my sons have tried to teach me, and I still sound like a teakettle.) but they can ease the way to finding work that works.

~~~~~~

Resources:

www.skillscan.net—Skill Scan is an on-line assessment or a card sort that can help you identify and articulate your skills.

www.elevateyourcareer.com—Elevations is an on-line career assessment tool or card sort that helps you explore your skills, values, personality, and career options.

www.novaworks.org/valuesdrivenwork—Values Driven Work is a values clarification tool.

www.authentichappiness.sas.upenn.edu—This free on-line VIA Signature Strengths Questionnaire was developed by psychologist Dr. Martin Seligman, author of *Authentic Happiness.*

Now, Discover Your Strengths, by Marcus Buckingham and Donald Clifton—This book includes a web-based strengths survey.
~~~~~~

From Transition to Transformation

I can still picture Mrs. Holman, my high school AP English teacher, impressing upon our class the importance of including transitions in our compositions. In fiction, transitions create tension, encouraging the reader to read on to find out how the plot thickens. In essays, a transition is required to smoothly bridge from one idea to the next. In our lives, transitions are periods that offer an opportunity for us to reinvent ourselves and our circumstances before we proceed to the next chapter of our life stories.

There are many types of life transitions. You'll likely experience quite a few over the course of your lifetime. Common transitions include: beginning school, graduating, moving, entering the workforce, getting married, having children, leaving and changing jobs, divorcing, being widowed, remarrying, and retiring. Some transitions are welcomed and chosen. Other transitions are unexpected and traumatic. Like breaking in new shoes, any change to the status quo takes some getting used to and is initially uncomfortable. But there can be wonderful opportunities in times of transition—opportunities for reexamination and renewal. Potential opportunities include:

Time to discover new possibilities
One of the most inspiring speakers I've ever heard is Benjamin Zander, the conductor of the Boston Philharmonic Orchestra. In his presentations, he draws an important distinction between someone in a downward spiral and someone who radiates possibility. An unemployed person in a downward spiral might complain, for example:

> *I was laid off this summer and really couldn't enjoy the weather or our family vacation because I was so worried about finding a job. I've only landed three interviews and haven't been asked back for any second interviews. There aren't many jobs out there, and I'm up against tons of more qualified applicants. Now we are heading into the holidays, so there will be even fewer companies hiring.*

Someone who radiates possibility might say:

> *I was burned out and had been miserable in my job for years, so in some ways, I welcomed being laid off. It's*

giving me a chance to find work that I enjoy. I'm discovering that I have no desire to return to the corporate world. I've always had a secret desire to open my own business. I now have a few ideas that I'm considering. I'm taking some classes on starting a small business and am doing informational interviews with people who've successfully run similar businesses. The possibilities are exciting!

- Do your stories take a downward spiral, or do you radiate possibility?

Time to get to know yourself

Self-discovery can provide needed clarity during a time of transition. Before jumping into figuring out the "what" and the "how" of your next chapter, get to know the "who," the main character, first. When you are clear about your values, know what needs drive you, and are confident about the strengths and talents you bring to the world, it's easier to recognize the environments, relationships, and careers that will fulfill you. There are many exercises, assessments, and books that can help you better understand yourself and the way you interact with the world. I've listed quite a few of my favorites on my website www.balancewithgrace.com and in "Work that Works."

Time to reexamine your life

Don't pass up this opportunity! Wouldn't you rather live your life on purpose, not by default? Spend time soul-searching, and be willing to take the time to reflect on questions that you can't immediately answer. Here are a few thought-provoking questions to journal about or ponder. Pay special attention to any question that keeps cropping up or preoccupies you:

- What do I really want?
- What opportunities exist at this time?
- What dreams have I given up on that I'd like to resurrect?
- What gift or talent am I not fully utilizing?
- What would I like to contribute to the world?
- What changes do I need to make to live a life of my choosing?

Time to ...

Notice that all the above opportunities begin with "time." A transition often feels like a lull. It may, in the case of graduating, becoming unemployed, or retiring, bring with it empty hours to fill. This could be the perfect opportunity to spend more time with your family, to volunteer in your church or community, to take a class, to clean up the basement or garden, or to complete nagging household projects. I know several unemployed people who have been home during the first few months with their newborns. Ten years from now they probably won't remember being frustrated with their job searches, but they'll surely remember the time spent bonding with their babies.

- How can you make the most of the time during your transition?

The only thing certain in life is change. Instead of kicking and screaming the next time you're faced with change, look for the opportunities and possibilities. Good luck moving from transition to transformation as you create your unique life story!

~~~~~~~~~~~~~~~~~~~~~~~~~~~~~~~~~~~~~~~

Resources:

LifeLaunch: A Passionate Guide to the Rest of Your Life, by Fredrick Hudson and Pamela D. McLean

The Art of Possibility, by Rosamund Stone Zander and Benjamin Zander

Seasons of Change: Using Nature's Wisdom to Grow Through Life's Inevitable Ups and Downs, by Carol McClellan
~~~~~~~~~~~~~~~~~~~~~~~~~~~~~~~~~~~~~~~

A Glowing Opportunity

Have you seen it yet? It's outta this world! Show times and locations vary, so be sure to check your local listings to find out when you can see it in your area. It's quite a spectacle!

I saw Mars for the first time back in 2003 when it was closer to the Earth than it had been for 59,619 years. It had been in the news for some time before I was ever able to catch a glimpse of it. Since we live in a wooded area, the only time I'd be able to see it from a window or our backyard would be around midnight, when its path would bring it directly overhead. I have enough trouble staying up until midnight on New Year's Eve, so I never seemed to be able to keep awake long enough to see it. I'd heard of people seeing the planet in the early morning, pre-dawn hours, but that didn't seem appealing either. Finally, driving home from a meeting one night at 9:00 p.m. it was there, glowing brightly. Mars was the only thing visible in the night sky except the occasional passing airplane. I felt giddy with excitement and had to continually remind myself to keep my eyes on the road as well as on Mars.

A few days later, on a crystal clear night during Labor Day weekend, my husband, in-laws, and I dragged ourselves away from the U.S. Open coverage to view Mars from the yard. I even roused my sleepy older son (the younger one wouldn't budge) to take a quick peek. We saw so many stars, even the Milky Way, but Mars appeared larger and brighter than everything but the moon. Our next door neighbor set up his telescope and invited us to take a closer look. At 90 X magnification we were able to spot dark storm clouds in the middle of Mars. We watched Mars move and had to reposition the telescope to keep Mars in sight.

Nearly missing this heavenly display made me consider all the other opportunities that we overlook. What have you missed out on because you were hesitant to go out of your way, to stick your neck out, or to deviate from your comfortable routine? With a little extra effort you could easily seize the opportunity to:

- pick fresh flowers for your home
- introduce yourself to a newcomer
- spend a few centering moments in meditation, prayer, or quiet

- open the door for someone who has his or her hands full
- experiment with a new recipe
- take the scenic route
- give a loved one your undivided attention

In the month of September, known for its return to routines, I challenge you to go against the grain and do something spontaneously out of the ordinary. Perhaps you'll end up "Mars-struck" like me or better. The possibilities are far-reaching!

Speak Your Dream

I'm a member of a small women's spirituality group that has been meeting for nearly a decade. The group gives us an opportunity to support and encourage one another as we explore and enrich our spiritual lives. I'm grateful to this special group of women for many gifts. I particularly appreciate the inspiration that the group provided for this piece and for the permission they gave me to share their stories.

At a brunch meeting of the group, after sharing great food and brief updates on each other's lives, our hostess led us through a reflective exercise. She passed around sheets of paper for us to record our responses to the following questions (and I invite you to take a few moments to do the same):

- If I had time, I would love to learn how to:
- If I didn't have to think about money I would:
- I always wished I had:
- After 9/11 I promised myself that I would:
- In the next year I will weave some of these things into my life by:

What happened next was fascinating. Over and over as we shared our wishes and dreams, someone else from the group would pipe up with a suggestion, an invitation, or a resource that suddenly made the dream feel within reach. Some examples of possibilities that opened up were:

- an offer of personal instruction for someone who wanted to learn how to cane furniture
- a suggestion to someone who's near public transportation and has a backyard pool to consider house-swapping as a way to afford a family trip to Italy
- a recommendation of art classes offered by a town's community services department for someone who wanted to take painting lessons

- a generous invitation to several of us who were interested in kayaking to use a double kayak on a local lake

Even after our meeting, the offers continued. One member who's been taking a portrait photography class asked for willing models. I was one of several who jumped at this chance. As a result, I was finally able to update the family photo on my website!

- What dreams are you keeping under wraps?
- What wish could you make known to someone other than your cat or dog?

I encourage you to speak your dream this week. Then stand back, and look for what opportunities open up as a result.

Abundant Harvest

I've always had a green thumb and have been growing herbs, perennials, and salad greens for decades. Several years ago I was offered the chance to have a large vegetable garden at a nearby horse farm. Now I know what it's like to experience an abundant harvest. As an over-eager, novice vegetable gardener, I underestimated the yield from squash plants. I planted, not one, but a dozen zucchini and summer squash plants in my first season. Between the exceptionally fertile soil (thanks to all the manure) and ample rainfall, we had a tremendous yield. One day that August, I picked over a dozen zucchini and had even more to pick the next day!

Now, every fall as I pick the last pumpkins and begin putting the garden to bed for the winter, I wistfully recall the summer's bounty. I remember the different ways we used our bumper crops. I realize that many of the ways I used my gifts from the garden would apply to all sorts of gifts—gifts of communication, athletic ability, handiwork talents, charisma, a way with the written word, a flair for style, and more. As you read this list, I encourage you to reflect upon your abundant gifts, how you are using them, and how you might share even more of them with others.

Share the wealth

I often leave offerings of veggies on the doorsteps of the horse farm's owner and caretakers. They share their land with me, and I am happy to share the harvest. Friends and neighbors also welcome the overflow. My coaching colleagues were once surprised when I brought a basket full of zucchini to a meeting. They took fourteen off of my hands that night! I've been tempted to set out a table at the end of my driveway offering freebies.

Capitalize

Some enterprising children in our neighborhood must have had the same issues with prolific zucchini because they set up a zucchini and lemonade stand. Maybe next year my boys will decide to do this. They might even have a competitive advantage since all of our produce is organically grown.

Preserve

A family can only consume so much squash, tomatoes, or basil in a week. By freezing and canning, many foods can be "put up" to enjoy in the middle of the winter. I bake and freeze zucchini chocolate chip bars, zucchini bread, and zucchini muffins. I also make pesto, pasta sauces, and herb vinegars.

Use it or lose it
Just as muscles lose their tone with inactivity, veggies will rot if left too long on the vine. I learned this the hard way with my cauliflower plants. One year the cauliflower heads were nearly ready to pick before our vacation. I held off, thinking they'd grow even more in a week's time. Unfortunately, it was a rainy week, and I returned to find the entire crop covered with a green, algae-like slime.

Be grateful
Although we both relish them, at times my husband groans when he hears we are having yet another zucchini dish for supper. I've had fun experimenting with new ways to use (or in my children's case, disguise) zucchini. Despite occasional periods of over-saturation, we all agree that homegrown vegetables are fun to plant, grow, and eat, and we look forward to the harvest.

I hope this has given you a few ideas for using your bountiful gifts. If one of your gifts is cooking and you have innovative zucchini recipes, please send them my way.

~~~~~~

Resources:

The Garden-Fresh Vegetable Cookbook, by Andrea Chesman
~~~~~~

Reclaiming Your Time

September is a month when everyone and everything seems to gear back up after the summer. Children don backpacks and return to school; grownups return to work, leaving the lazy days of vacation or long weekends behind. Sports teams, clubs, committees, and professional organizations that may have suspended their meetings and practices over the summer are back in full swing. Many people find the cooler temperatures invigorating and welcome the quicker pace. But others feel like digging in their heels and stubbornly shouting "Whoa!" when they see how much is now on their plates. If this latter description fits you, even slightly, read on for some suggestions for reclaiming control of your time.

Look at how you are spending your time
Keep a time log for a typical weekday. You'll gather even more valuable information if you keep records for an entire week. Note how much time you spend in all of your activities, including sleeping, grooming, exercise, working, running errands, preparing and eating meals, watching TV, reading, and checking email. At the end of the day or week, create a pie chart of how you spent your time. Are you surprised by where your time went? Compare this pie chart to the ideal workday and ideal weekend charts you created on page 22. Did you allocate your time in the way you prefer?

Reexamine your priorities
What do you most want to devote your time and energy to at this point in your life? Make a list, and narrow down to the three to five things that are most important to you. These are your top priorities. Refer back to your pie chart to see how much of your time is engaged in activities that are important to you. What steps could you take to make your schedule more reflective of your true priorities?

Make choices based on your priorities
There's something about suddenly realizing that you have meetings three or four weeknights in a row that makes you reconsider your commitments. At times I've had three events fall on the same night. Since I don't have the Time-Turner that Hermione uses in *Harry Potter and the Prisoner of Azkaban* to magically turn back the clock so that she can be in two places at

the same time, I've been forced to make choices. Knowing your priorities will make this type of decision-making easier. It can also help to:

- set and stick to limits. In our family, the limit is one sport per child per season.
- divide and conquer. Have your spouse or a friend fill you in on what happened in a meeting.
- say, "No." If it doesn't fall into your top priorities, it isn't something you want to do, or if it would push you over the edge into overwhelm, pass on it.
- schedule what's important. Treat family dinners or exercise sessions the same way you would a business meeting. Enter them in your calendar, and work around them.
- make adjustments as needed to make your life work for you. My limit used to be two evening meetings a week. As I've worked to finish this book, I further reduced that in order to preserve more productive energy for writing.

We are each given twenty-four hours each day. As the anniversary of September 11 reminds us, we can never be certain how many days and years we have left. Choose wisely to make the most of every moment!

Take Back Your Time

There's a not so well-known U.S. and Canadian holiday on October 24 that's well worth celebrating. It's Take Back Your Time Day. The goal of Take Back Your Time Day is to build awareness of the time poverty created by our current work/life imbalance and to begin public conversation about what to do about it.

The sad statistics

Take Back Your Time Day is held on October 24, the date by which most Americans have put in as many work hours as the average Western European worker puts in during the course of a year. Between 1973 and 2000, the average American worker added 199 work hours to the annual total of time spent at work. The U.S. has no minimum vacation time, and 26% of working Americans, according to a Boston College survey, take no vacation over the course of a year. According to the International Labor Organization (ILO), 80% of men and 62% of women work more than 40 hours a week. A *U.S. New and World Reports* statistic shows that close to 40% of Americans workers log more than 50 hours a week. A lack of mandatory paid family leave and no cap on mandatory overtime push many American workers to the limit. The slogan from a Take Back Your Time Day T-shirt: "Medieval Peasants Worked Less Than You Do" certainly raises questions about our current quality of life![7]

Lack of time off has significant ramifications for our health, families, and communities. The ubiquitous complaints of "no time to cook" and "no time to exercise" contribute to over half of the U.S. population being overweight and the increasing rates of obesity. Busy, hurried parents model an overworked, underplayed lifestyle for their children. We are producing a generation of kids who are overscheduled and under-connected. My boys are frequently frustrated with how difficult it is to hook up with friends after school because of conflicting activities and sports schedules. Late nights at the office and busy after-school schedules mean fewer families are gathering around the supper table. They are missing the chance to nourish their bodies with good food and their hearts with conversation with loved ones. Between the demands of work and family, many find it difficult to make time to volunteer and may even feel too busy to vote.

What's a busy person to do about it? Here are some thoughts:

Create windows of time
The Boston area Take Back Your Time movement joined with the Mass Council of Churches www.masscouncilofchurches.org to develop a Take Four Windows of Time campaign. The campaign encourages people to set aside four blocks of time between Labor Day and Take Back Your Time Day on October 24 to slow down and spend some time in restorative, life-enriching activities. For a list of 50 Plus Pretty Quick Things You Can Do visit: www.simpleliving.net/timeday/campaign-materials.asp. For some additional seasonal suggestions, consider one or more of the following activities:

- make Halloween decorations or costumes
- play a favorite card or board game
- play your favorite music, and dance around your living room
- walk in the woods, and collect leaves
- plant spring bulbs
- go apple picking
- enjoy some pumpkin pie or mulled cider

Take political action
Your efforts can help support the Take Back Your Time legislative program to:

- make Election Day a national holiday
- enact paid Family and Medical Leave as part of the Family and Medical Leave Act
- enact three weeks' minimum annual paid leave for all workers
- enact a cap on mandatory overtime

You could create a petition and collect signatures as a first step to getting these items on a ballot. For a sample letter of endorsement you can use to get the attention and support of your public officials visit www.simpleliving.net/timeday/engage-resolution.asp.

Mastermind solutions
Don't suffer in silence about your lack of time. Strike up conversations with friends, neighbors, and colleagues to find out what others are experiencing and how they are coping. But don't let complaints turn your brainstorming session into a pity party. Keep the dialog productive by asking open-ended questions that explore solutions. Some of the best questions begin with "what"

or "how," such as, "What would be ideal?" and "How could you do things differently?"

Help the Take Back Your Time Day holiday and concept take hold in your community. Mark your calendar today, and plan a fun, relaxing way to celebrate. I bet you've got the time coming to you!

~~~~~~

Resources:

www.timeday.org—Visit this site to learn more about the holiday and this non-partisan coalition for change.

Fighting Overwork and Time Poverty in America, by John de Graf, editor

Work to Live: The Guide to Getting a Life, by Joe Robinson

Timeshifting: Creating More Time to Enjoy Your Life, by Stephen Rechtshaffen
~~~~~~

Don't Be a Busy Body!

Are you a busy body? No, I'm not asking if you are nosy and have to know everyone else's business! I mean are you someone who's always doing something? Are you one of those bodies that tends to stay in motion from the time you wake up until the time you crash at night? If someone you haven't seen in a while asks you how you've been, is your response usually "Busy!"? Do your conversations sound like contests to see who's busier, as you and others take turns reeling off all that's on your plates, on your schedules, and on your to-do lists? It's no coincidence that each of these phrases contains the word "on." Busy bodies are always *on*. How does that end up playing out in our lives?

There are certainly payoffs that we get from our busy-ness. (And in case you are wondering, I can be quite a busy body.) When we accomplish a lot, we feel good being productive. We may thrive on the acknowledgment we get from others when they marvel, "Wow! How do you manage to get so much done?" Being "on" forces us to be "up" as well. Keeping busy can easily distract us from things that are bothering us. There's simply no time to think. We get a charge and a rush of energy from the adrenaline that courses through our body when we run late or come up against a deadline.

But there's a price to busy-ness as well. Although adrenaline can save your life, giving you the energy you need in fight-or-flight situations, a steady diet of it is not ideal. Eventually this may result in any number of stress-induced dis-eases. At times you may feel scattered and disoriented from the dizzying whirl of activities and commitments. Perhaps it feels like you are on one of those spinning teacups rides at an amusement park. The speed and the sickening swirl may make you want to shout, "Stop! I want to get off." The good news is that you are not at the mercy of the ride operator; *you* are the one in control of your life.

If you'd like to find ways to stop or at least slow down the ride, you can manage your busy-ness with these four steps (which together form the easy-to-remember acronym "busy").

Breathe

A reader emailed me in response to a newsletter I wrote about peace. She wrote that she enjoyed the article and would like to find peace but that she didn't know how. There were a number of possible suggestions that occurred to me, but I decided that, rather than overwhelming her with options, I'd share one simple step. I replied that taking slower, deeper breaths was one of the best ways to feel more peaceful and balanced. When we feel stressed our breathing quickens and gets shallower. We end up using only a fraction of our lung capacity. Breath is considered the outward manifestation of the vital life force known in the East as *Prana*, *Chi*, or *Qi*. Breathing is something you have to do anyway, so why not take full, deep breaths to bring all of you to what you do? You'll find that when you become more mindful of your breath, you become more mindful of everything.

Also, give yourself breathing room in your day. Even with a full schedule, if you allow a buffer around each of your commitments, you won't feel frantic or rushed. In the space between, you can take a few slow, mindful breaths.

Unhook

George de Mestral, the Swiss engineer, was inspired by cockleburs in his invention of Velcro.[8] If you've ever gotten burrs stuck to your socks or clothing, you know that they have staying power. Each strand of a burr has a hook at the end, which helps it securely latch onto things. If you closely examine Velcro, you'll notice that one side is made up of a mass of hooks while the other side sports a mass of loops that the hooks cling to.

For those of us who are inclined to busy-ness, it sometimes seems that we are wearing a Velcro suit and that every project, every item on our to do list, and every concern has a hook extending out towards us, firmly attaching to our suit. Even when we are not busy with our projects and concerns, they cling to us, sapping our thoughts and energy. The busier we are, the more hooks we have, and the harder it becomes to move freely. We may pride ourselves on our multi-tasking ability. If we are honest, however, we recognize what studies are beginning to show—that multi-tasking is not productive. There are a number of ways to unhook:

- complete unfinished business
- prioritize and postpone projects that aren't urgent
- delegate whenever possible

- carefully consider new commitments, and don't be afraid to say, "No"
- focus on only one thing at a time.

Self nurture

Are there things you want to do for yourself that keep being crowded out by things you feel you should do for others? If this becomes a habit, with your needs and wants always coming in last place, if at all, then you are heading for trouble. I recently heard a powerful quote from a 12-step program: "Give from your excess, not from your essence." If you take steps to replenish and keep your cup full, there will be plenty to go around, for both you and others. Apply the financial planning strategy: "Pay yourself first," to your self-care. That way you'll ensure you aren't depleted or overdrawn. A number of my clients begin their day with a "Power Hour"—time that's spent in prayer or meditation, journaling, setting intentions, reading, movement, and self-care. Even if you can't begin your day with an entire hour of self-nurture, identify the practices that keep you at your best, and make them habits.

You

Underneath all the busy-ness is a precious treasure—you! As you clear away some of the busy-ness, you begin to rediscover and reconnect with *you*. You may have forgotten who you are at the core, underneath all the roles, responsibilities, trappings, and travails that make up your busy-ness. Up to now you may have created a lifestyle that keeps you in the doing mode. As you begin to breathe and allow for breathers, unhook, and nurture yourself, you'll find yourself shifting away from always doing to being. From this undistracted, expansive being place, it's easier to know what's important to you and to make choices that are aligned with who you are.

~~~~~~

Resources:

Succeeding as a Super Busy Parent, by Natalie Gahrmann

Meditations for Women Who Do Too Much, by Anne Wilson Schaef
~~~~~~

Dinner Invitation

What are you doing the evening of September 24th? I'd like to invite you to dine, not with me and other readers, although that certainly would be fun, but with your family. If you live alone, I invite you to have dinner with a companion other than the television. The fourth Monday of September is designated as Family Day—A Day to Eat Dinner with Your Children.™ CASA, Columbia University's National Center on Addiction and Substance Abuse launched Family Day in 2001 because their research consistently showed that the more frequently children eat dinner with their families, the less likely they are to smoke, drink, or use drugs.

"CASA's 2006 report *The Importance of Family Dinners III* found that compared to kids who have fewer than three family dinners per week, children and teens who have 5-7 family dinners per week are:

- at 70 percent lower risk for substance abuse
- half as likely to try cigarettes or marijuana
- one third less likely to try alcohol
- half as likely to get drunk monthly

Kids who frequently eat dinner with their families are also likelier to have better grades and confide in their parents."[9]

In our family, we've found that our teenager will open up most around the dinner table and talk about what's going on at school, in sports, and on the social scene. He's just entered his sophomore year, and so far (Knock on wood!) he's managing to stay out of trouble.

Although it's not always easy, here are some ways to sit down to regular family dinners:

1. Find the time.

Family dinners often don't just happen; they require planning. It's easiest to eat dinner at the same time every evening. When I was growing up, my family ate together every evening at 5:30 p.m. Sometimes for fun, my mother would ring a bell or call "Suey!" (a common way to call pigs for their food) to round us up. She didn't need to summon us. We were all programmed to be home and sitting down to eat at 5:30 p.m.

Times have changed, at least in our household. As a two-income family with everyone except me involved in team sports, our schedules aren't so predictable. In this case, at the beginning of the week, perhaps over a Sunday evening family dinner, talk about what everybody's schedule is for the coming week. Figure out which nights you'll eat together and at what time. Ask for everyone's commitment to being there.

2. Plan appealing meals.

One barrier to family dinners is the difficulty in finding foods that everyone will eat. In most families there's usually at least one picky eater. The way we've dealt with that is to prepare meals that can be either plain or fancy. For instance, pasta (Barilla's PLUS high protein pasta is a staple in our house.) could be served plain or with a little butter or olive oil and cheese on top with steamed broccoli on the side for the finicky eater. The rest could top their pasta with a scallop broccoli pasta sauce made from the remaining broccoli. We encourage our picky eater to try small bites of unfamiliar foods. Over time he's gradually beginning to expand his repertoire.

To expedite meal planning, keep a list of meals that are hits and another list of dishes to try. In the Resources section, I've listed a few of my favorite sources for quick and delicious recipes.

3. Enjoy the company.

Minimize distractions so that you can fully focus on enjoying the food and each other. Turn off the TV, and don't answer the phone or respond to instant messages during mealtimes. Be curious, and ask questions that encourage others to share their thoughts, feelings, and experiences. If you know that certain questions such as "What happened at school today?" tend to elicit "Nothing." as the response, be more creative with your questions. For instance, you could ask:

- What's the funniest thing that happened at school today?
- What's your favorite class so far, and why?
- Who are you getting to know better this year?

If you need some extra help, *Food for Talk,* available through www.foodfortalk.net, is a whimsically decorated file box chock full of provocative prompts. Their mission is: "bringing families together one conversation at a time." Amen to that!

~~~~~~

Resources:

Eating Well magazine is full of healthy, uncomplicated recipes, many of which can be found in their recipe archives on www.eatingwell.com.

www.epicurious.com—I often use this archive of recipes from *Gourmet* and *Bon Appetit* when I'm entertaining or planning special meals.

The Moosewood Restaurant Cooks at Home: Fast and Easy Recipes for Any Day or other cookbooks by Mollie Katzen
~~~~~~

Between Ease and Effort

I remember when Sue Richards, my favorite yoga teacher, started teaching at our health club. She used a few phrases and instructional cues that I'd never heard before but really liked. One that particularly stood out for me was "Find a place between ease and effort." What a perfect prompt! I liked having permission to listen to my body, to find the depth in a posture that I could sustain without strain, knowing I could back off if needed. This encouraged me to stretch, while exploring the edge. In the case of a couple of poses, such as the headstand and backbend, this approach eventually led me to surprising places beyond my perceived limit.

Aside from a yoga practice, there are plenty of other areas in life where it could be helpful to make modifications to find a place between ease and effort. Work, relationships, spirituality, community service, homemaking, personal growth, health, and wellness, are a few that come to mind. Which areas are calling out for your attention? More effort may be required to keep from stagnating in some of these areas. It's good to be comfortable, yet not complacent. Pick an area of your life and consider:

- What feels neglected, stale, or uninspired?
- What's the underlying potential here?
- What could bring new energy to this?
- What steps are you willing to take to explore new possibilities?

Feeling overwhelmed is practically epidemic, so I'm guessing there probably are other areas of your life that feel all-consuming. You may need to lessen the pace or ease up on the intensity to feel better. Consider an area or two where you are expending tremendous effort:

- What makes you feel stretched to the limit?
- What would feel better?
- What could make a dramatic difference?
- What committed action will move you in the desired direction?

As you and your family transition from the end of summer back into a fall work or school schedule, I invite you to examine your life circumstances with fresh eyes and make adjustments to find your ideal place between ease and effort.

~~~~~~

Resources:

www.yogamahout.com—My yoga teacher, Susan Richards, offers a terrific *Yoga Fitness Journal*.
~~~~~~

Life is Precious

Last October I received an unusual voice mail message. I had to replay it several times before I understood it. The woman spoke so quickly that at first I couldn't make out where she was calling from. I thought she said "North Andover Department," but I wasn't sure. On the fourth try I realized that she was calling from the "Mammography Department." I'd had a mammogram the day before. The phone call concerned me. Usually I don't hear anything and then I get a postcard a week later informing me that my mammogram was normal. This was my first digital mammogram. The technician told me that this technology makes it easier for radiologists to read films and spot problems in younger women. When I returned the call, I discovered that they wanted me to go back in for another mammogram.

After hearing this, as much as I believe in the power of positive thinking, it was hard not to let my mind travel to scary, "what if" places. My mom had breast cancer, even though, like me, she's always taken good care of herself with regular exercise, a healthy diet, and attention to work/life balance. Thankfully, with early detection, a lumpectomy, and radiation, she's been cancer-free for over ten years. It made me recall a poem she wrote during her treatment, which she's given me permission to share:

THE BUTTERFLY I FOUND IN SPRING

One day in spring
I found a yellow butterfly
with markings of black, rust, and blue.
I placed it in a small box
its severed wing
close to where it once belonged.

Now, as summer nudges fall,
I think about the way
mortality sometimes brushes up
against us, swift and silent
as velvety wings.

Copyright 1996 Frances Norton Honich

I went in the next day for several more mammography views and an ultrasound, which helped determine immediately that the suspicious area in my left breast was a cyst. Getting off of the examining table, I blinked back tears of relief and thankfulness. Driving back home, it was as if the world suddenly turned Technicolor. The sky never looked so blue; the colors of the turning leaves never looked so brilliant. I was flooded with gratefulness for life. I was even grateful for this scare since it gave me an opportunity to reconsider and recommit to the priorities in my life.

October is Breast Cancer Awareness month. Women, if you are over forty or have a family history of breast cancer, please keep up-to-date with your diagnostic screenings: mammograms and/or thermography and monthly self-exams.

The end of this month also marks the end of Daylight Savings Time for many of us. We are reminded when we set our clocks back to check and change the batteries in smoke and carbon dioxide detectors. Let's also use this as a reminder to do what's needed to keep our own batteries charged. For instance, if there are doctor, dental, or eye appointments you've been meaning to schedule, do so. Or if there's another commitment to your wellness you've wanted to make: joining a gym, actually going to the gym, eating well, scheduling down time, do that. Don't wait for a wake-up call. Take steps, now, to preserve what's precious—your life.

~~~~~~

Resources:

www.thermography.com—Visit this site to learn more about early detection infrared imaging and find a center near you.

Dr. Susan Love's Breast Book, by Susan M. Love, Karen Lindsey, and Marcia Williams
~~~~~~

Putting Things By

As the leaves turn and fall, squirrels and chipmunks are busy putting food by. They scamper around burying acorns and seeds, building up their food supply for the winter months ahead. As someone who often struggles to find my car in large parking lots, I marvel at these animals' ability to locate underground stores.

I, too, find myself bustling around, doing my best to preserve the last of my garden's bounty. In the past weeks I've made and stocked my freezer with herb butter, spaghetti sauce, applesauce, pumpkin puree, and zucchini bread. I have a distant memory of my grandmother's well-stocked pantry shelves. They were lined with glass Ball canning jars of applesauce, jams, jellies, pickles, and preserved peaches. With the global economy and efficient transportation systems that ensure a constant supply of fresh produce, there's not the same necessity to put food by as there was years ago. I doubt if any new homes come equipped with a root cellar. Maybe I'm old-fashioned, or maybe it's a byproduct of the practical, frugal, Puritanical heritage passed on to me from my maternal lineage, but I enjoy putting things by. I love having a taste of summer in the middle of winter. Extra food stores make me feel well-prepared to weather winter storms. I also like having a surplus of homemade goodies to share with friends, neighbors, and holiday hostesses.

As we approach All Souls Day, a day set aside on November 2 to honor the dead, I encourage you to recognize and give thanks for the gifts preserved and passed on to you from departed loved ones. My aforementioned grandmother, for instance, passed on her love of teaching, reading, spiritual study, and stillness. She also taught me how to crochet, how to scout for treasures at tag sales, and how to play a mean game of Spite and Malice. There are material gifts I inherited as well: her china, a vintage treadle sewing machine, and a braided rug she'd made using strips from old wool coats purchased at tag sales. All of these things help to keep my memories of her alive and contribute to the feeling I often have of her watching over me.

Take a moment to reflect on the contributions you are now making that will be remembered by those close to you:

- o What legacy are you leaving?
- o How will the world be a better place because of your time spent here?
- o How are you making a mark?
- o What gifts do you have yet to contribute?
- o What's the best way to pass these on?

Here are some ideas to consider:

- ➢ acknowledging others through praise, encouragement, thank-you notes, testimonials, and birthday letters
- ➢ keeping journals to record insight, growth, and the adventures of daily life
- ➢ writing a book—someday I hope my boys and the future generations of my family will appreciate this book
- ➢ creating a photo album for each family member
- ➢ teaching what you know, whether it's how to cook, build a birdhouse, prune shrubs, or speak another language
- ➢ tape recording stories of your life
- ➢ producing a video to capture your voice and your presence
- ➢ pouring out your creativity through any type of art form: painting, crafts, poetry, music
- ➢ inventing something totally unique
- ➢ working with a financial professional on estate planning
- ➢ making or updating your will
- ➢ documenting where important records are stored
- ➢ planning your own funeral or memorial service, choosing readings and music that leave a message

Take a lesson from the squirrels, and tuck something away now to brighten the bleakness of the coming winter. While you're at it, determine what you'd like to preserve for the future. Begin to create or add to a legacy that will benefit others long after you've passed.

After the Fall

As much as we aim for balance in our lives, there are times when we fall. I was reminded of this fact when, in the span of a week, both my dad and my niece took bad falls. My seventy-year-old father, who takes medication that makes him rather unsteady, fell at a local airport. My niece, who is quite an athlete, tripped at volleyball practice over a pair of shoes someone had left courtside. Fortunately, my dad suffered only bruises, scrapes, and wounded pride. My niece tore several muscles, which took several weeks to heal. We are all grateful that the injuries weren't more serious.

These are physical falls, but there are other ways we "crash" as well. There are highs and lows in everyone's life. Many women, for instance, experience cyclical mood swings relating to hormonal fluctuations. I know I've had my share of monthly meltdowns, which a client once referred to as "kitchen floor moments." Both men and women are susceptible to disappointments and emotional lows when work, family, or life circumstances fall short of their expectations.

The next time you are physically or figuratively on the floor, here are some ways to right yourself and bounce back:

Survey the situation
Before you immediately hop up and spring back into action, take a moment to inventory the damage. In some cases you can cause further injury by moving or bearing weight on a limb. If you ignore the cause of an emotional upset, your attempts to regain your equilibrium may fail as you grasp at immediate, stop-gap measures rather than long-term, effective, solutions.

Get back up
Down isn't a place you want to stay for too long. Don't be shy about asking for assistance. Be gentle with yourself. You probably feel fragile and somewhat vulnerable, so take your time with this. You may need someone to help pull you up and someone to lean on as you start moving. Brush yourself off. Blow your nose. If you've been crying, splash cold water on your face.

Get professional help if needed
Broken bones, dislocations, torn ligaments, and concussions all require medical diagnosis and treatment. Some emotional upsets require intervention as well. Ten percent of the U.S. population suffers from depression. If healing or medication is needed, a therapist or psychiatrist can be lifesaving. If it's sorting out, strategizing, and taking action that you need, a coach can be of tremendous help.

Recuperate with "RICE"
With a number of strains and sprains in our household over the years, I've learned how effective RICE—rest, ice, compression, and elevation—is in the recipe for recovery. It also works well for bruised spirits.

REST—An injured muscle will heal itself, but it needs time off of the job to mend. This is the perfect time for extra TLC (tender loving care). Give yourself ample time before you attempt your usual level of activity. We tend to lose both heart and perspective when we've stretched ourselves beyond our limits to reach a breaking point. A good night's sleep can work wonders. If it's hours to go before bedtime, rest by taking a nap, meditating, or closing your eyes to block out the world for a few minutes.

ICE—Applying an ice pack can help you minimize pain, bruising, and swelling from inflammation. The sooner you ice an injury, the better. Similarly, any type of stress reduction or "chilling out" is balm for the soul.

COMPRESSION—Sometimes an Ace bandage is wrapped around an injury to control swelling. Likewise, you'll want to look for measures that soothe, rather than inflame an emotional state. Since it's not healthy to suppress emotions, when I sense clients need to vent, I'll ask if they need a BMW—short for Bi*ch, Moan, and Whine—session. I do ask my clients to limit these to five minutes. Once the steam of anger, resentment, and upset has been released, it's easier to see more clearly and switch the focus from problems to solutions.

ELEVATE—Raising an injured limb above heart level reverses the flow of blood and can minimize swelling. Look for ways to comfortably prop yourself up, perhaps with pillows. By the same token, if you are feeling down, find ways to bolster your spirits. Dancing, reading something inspirational, getting some fresh air, or listening to uplifting music such as Josh Groban's *You Raise Me Up* seem to do the trick for me.

Get support.
You may need some additional support as you move forward after a fall. Crutches, a walking stick, or a brace can help if there's been a physical injury. In the case of emotional dips, you may need to ask for help. If you feel like the weight of the world is on your shoulders, find someone to share the load. If you are overwhelmed by trying to do it all, enlist help. For example, if you are the one who planned, shopped for, and cooked a meal, ask others pitch in to clean up afterwards.

Learn from the experience
If you know what caused your fall—an obstacle, uneven terrain, improper technique, or a slippery surface—you can do your best to avoid it in the future. If you can identify what triggered your upset, you can take steps to remedy the current situation and prevent a reoccurrence.

Early Winter and Holidays

Content with Enough

In November of 2006 I attended a mind-expanding ICF coaching conference in St. Louis. One of the inspiring keynote presenters was Lynne Twist, the author of *The Soul of Money: Transforming Your Relationship with Money and Life*. A powerful message of hers, which I think is particularly good food for thought during the period between Thanksgiving and the holidays is:

"We no longer have a relationship with enough, only with more."

On Thanksgiving, a holiday where we celebrate the harvest and our bounty with a plentiful feast, it's easy to eat more than our fill. Babies naturally know when to stop nursing or feeding. Like a gas station pump, they automatically shut off when full. Most of us have lost this ability. Either we're not aware of being full, or we choose to ignore the signals and opt for more. Consuming more than we need doesn't happen just on holidays. It's become a way of life.

To moderate your food consumption:

Have a drink of water
Sometimes we think we are hungry when what we really are is thirsty. Drinking water between and before meals will help curb your appetite.

Use smaller dishes
Most of us were taught to clean our plates, and we often feel guilty if we don't. This becomes a problem when we fill big dishes with large portions. Opt for smaller plates and bowls. You'll feel satisfied with less.

Share an entrée
Many restaurant portions are enormous, easily serving two. If dining alone, ask to be served a half portion with the remainder wrapped up to go.

Reserve serving dishes for entertaining
It's easy to go for second helpings when food is passed family style. You'll have less temptation (and fewer dishes to wash) if you must return to the kitchen for more.

Portion out snacks
We are apt to eat mindlessly and eat more when eating straight from a bag or box. Put an individual serving of chips, crackers, or other snack food into a bowl, so you'll know when to stop.

Brush your teeth
If you want to cut out late night snacks, get in the habit of flossing and brushing your teeth right after dinner. You'll think twice about that treat if you know you'll have to brush up again.

Food's hardly the only area of excess in our society. What about all of our *stuff*? Once while teaching a church school class, we were asked to make a group list of some of our material possessions. I was embarrassed to confess that we have eight phones and four computers for a household of four. (We do have separate lines for two home-based businesses, but still, this is a lot.) Our inventory was a dramatic contrast to a photo we saw in a book of an African family with their limited possessions lined up in front of their small home. We all came away with a greater appreciation for all that we have.

Sadly, what we have isn't always satisfying. Author and blogger, Dan Pink, another one of our conference keynote presenters, spoke about the "Abundance Gap." Over the last half-century, the level of prosperity in the U.S. has risen dramatically but the level of satisfaction hasn't. We may be three times as rich, but we aren't any happier.

Lynne Twist made another point, which could go far towards helping us close that gap. She said,

"The only route to abundance is through the doorway of enough."

Before making purchases, consider:

- Do you want this or need this?
- Why do you want or need this?
- What do you already own or have access to that could serve the same purpose?
- What would feel like enough?

Let's be mindful of our blessings, and learn to recognize when enough's enough!

~~~~~~

Resources:

The Soul of Money: Transforming Your Relationship with Money and Life, by Lynne Twist

A Whole New Mind: Why Right-Brainers Will Rule the Future, by Daniel H. Pink

Gratitude: A Way of Life, by Louise Hay and friends
~~~~~~

To Your Health

As we head towards the holidays, it seems like so many people are either sick, fighting a cold, or getting over a bug. Even I, who rarely succumb to colds, have sometimes begun the season under the weather. One year beginning the weekend before Thanksgiving, I had aches, chills, and headache from a fever that lasted three days. My sore throat and low energy level lasted even longer than that. I was happy to be well enough to travel and celebrate Thanksgiving with family. When we went around the table telling what we were most grateful for, I expressed heartfelt thanks for the gift of health. I'd like to share with you some ideas for protecting that gift so that you may have a happy, healthy holiday.

Listen to your body
One of the reasons that I'm hardly ever sick is that I pay attention to and heed my body's signals. Swollen or tender glands are the warning signs I usually get. If I rest more by spending a half hour napping or reading on the coach and get to bed early, I'm usually able to fight off whatever is threatening.

- What are your typical warning signs?
- What is your body asking you to do?

Balance work with rest
I usually don't work at all on the weekends. I use weekends to recharge, play, and do projects around the house and gardens. That particular year I attended a coaching conference in Quebec the first weekend of November, taught a class in Boston the following Saturday, and for the third Saturday, was scheduled to drive out to my sister-in-law's house. I planned to spend the day sewing bedroom curtains, to honor the gift certificate I'd given the previous Christmas. My sister-in-law had to take a rain check. If there's no downtime in the schedule, illness often forces it.

- How much downtime will you have this week?
- What do you need to say "yes" or "no" to in order to feel balanced?

Monitor your stress level
There's a fine line between anxiety and excitement, and I often dance right along the edge of it. That year I was about to launch

my first product, *Success with Grace*, which is a practice-building program for coaches. The CD sets were ready to go, but I kept adding to and editing the e-book. Although it was exciting to be in the home stretch of a big project, I felt the stress of meeting my deadline in the midst of holiday preparations.

- What is currently causing you stress?
- How can you manage or better yet, minimize, stress?

Maintain healthy habits
I know what nurturing practices support my health and keep me at my best. I've ingrained them as habits, however, every now and then a change in weather, routine, or circumstances derails me. That's no problem as long as I quickly get back on track. Sometimes a lapse sets off a domino effect and if not curtailed can lead to "dis-ease." For instance, I didn't get outside to exercise as much as usual during the coaching conference. This prevented me from sleeping as much or as well as usual. To boost my lagging energy, I ate sugar, which made me crave more. This unhealthy combination weakened my resistance. It's no wonder I got sick. Once I recovered I got back into the groove and returned to my healthy habits of:

- exercise
- enough sleep/rest
- journaling
- meditation
- fresh air/sunshine/being in nature
- romance/touch
- healthy eating
- taking vitamins/supplements
- fun/laughter
- relaxing/ "couch time"

These strategies can help you enjoy a happy, healthy holiday season.

- What nurturing habits (from page 48) do you want to reinstate?
- What will help you maintain these practices, especially over the holidays?

Holiday Balance

Do you consider "holiday balance" an oxymoron? If decorating, shopping, baking, and entertaining now fill up your free time, balance may seem elusive—something to save for your New Year's wish list. I believe it not only *is* possible to enjoy balance during December, but in fact, it's also a key ingredient to a happy holiday. The secret, as perfectly demonstrated by a circus tightrope walker, is to make small shifts and slight adjustments when necessary. This time of year it may take more frequent adjustments to maintain balance. Here are some suggestions to help keep you on your high wire.

Make a list and check it twice

Feeling preoccupied by the long list of to-do's vying for attention in your brain? Committing the list to paper can help you better focus on the here-and-now. Write down all the things you plan to do between now and New Year's. Include: shopping (specifically whom you need to buy for and what you plan to give), wrapping, mailing gifts, sending cards, visits, travel, baking, entertaining, decorating, and attending parties, church services, school, and community activities. Now go back over your list with a discerning eye, asking:

- What are the most important activities?
- What are you eager to do?
- What activities do you dread?
- Where could you relax certain expectations?
- How could you simplify holiday preparations?

This year, for example, I plan to make only a couple batches of cookies and will buy others from bake sales and church bazaars. I'll also do more on-line shopping and will print address labels instead of hand addressing holiday cards. (No one can read my handwriting, anyway!).

Focus on meaningful traditions

Look at your list, and identify the traditions that have meaning for you. Holiday preparations are often dictated by what we've done in the past or what our parents did when we were growing up.

- What traditions would you like to hold on to?
- What would you like to let go of?
- What new traditions would you like to create?

Candlelight services, musical and theatrical performances, special stories and meals, can connect us to Spirit and remind us of what we are celebrating in the first place. Keep what's meaningful for you in your holiday plans, and curtail what isn't.

Take care of yourself

Most of us know what we need to do to keep ourselves at our best. There's a certain minimum requirement of exercise, natural light, healthy food, and rest that our bodies crave. This is an important time to honor those needs. Colds and flu tend to peak after the holidays. Colder weather often keeps us indoors where we are exposed to more germs. We are also more susceptible to illness when we are run down. Be especially gentle with yourself if the holidays are a sad time for you and if you are still healing from a recent loss.

Keep the joy in your heart

Have you ever tried to write all your holiday cards in one sitting? If so, you probably ended up with a horrible case of writer's cramp and felt like Scrooge himself. Pace yourself so you don't hit the wall. Imagine that your internal Joy-o-meter™ (see page 50) automatically triggers a cut-off switch as soon as you stop having fun. The only way you can resume your activity is by finding a way to make it enjoyable again, perhaps by listening to some favorite music, or enlisting a helper. Or take a break, and come back later, after you've eaten or rested.

Balance consumption with charity

There's been a tremendous outpouring of donations to help those suffering in the aftermath of September 11 and hurricane Katrina. It's heartwarming to see how we've rallied to take care of those who have been personally affected by these tragedies. During the colder months it's more important than ever for the haves to share with the have-nots.

- How well do your checkbook entries reflect your personal values?
- How would you like to support those who are less fortunate?

If you'd like to do more, consider making a gift donation in someone's name, dropping off canned or packaged goods to a local food pantry, volunteering at a soup kitchen, donating outgrown outerwear, and writing a tax-deductible check to your favorite charity.

Indulge moderately
When faced with tempting treats, lavish spreads, and free flowing wine, it takes ironclad willpower to say no. Unless you know that that one drink or one sweet will turn into a binge, it's fine to be decadent occasionally. To keep from going overboard, take tiny samples of everything on a buffet, split a dessert with a friend, and pour only half a glass at a time. The best strategy is to know and stick to your limits. If you overdo it despite your best intentions, forgive yourself, and start anew the next day.

Lie fallow
This is rest time in the natural world. Deciduous trees take a break from photosynthesis. Newly planted bulbs slowly send down roots to support future blooms.

- How can you mirror the natural cycle in your own life?
- How do you find stillness?

Especially if you have a whirl of social activities on tap for December, allow plenty of down time to recharge. How about taking a long winter's nap, curling up with a good book, gazing into a roaring fire, or meditating? Couch time, quiet time, and vacation time can be wonderfully restoring.

Here's to a happy, balanced holiday!

Preparing for Happy Holidays

For some, the period from Thanksgiving through New Year's is the highlight of the year, a time to celebrate with family and friends, give thanks for abundance, share with others, and reconnect spiritually. For many, however, it's a stressful time, as already full schedules nearly burst with the additional work of entertaining, shopping, wrapping, mailing, baking, and decorating. If you'd like to maximize the joy and minimize the stress in your holiday celebrations this year, careful planning can make all the difference.

Begin now by reflecting upon what aspects of past celebrations you'd like to keep and which ones you'd like to modify. Look over old calendars and any saved lists to remind you of the typical holiday preparations, travel, social events, spending, and volunteer commitments that accompany this time of year.

- What family customs and religious or ethnic traditions are a part of your celebrations?
- What behind-the-scenes orchestration is involved in creating the holiday magic?
- How is the work divvied up?
- Which aspects have lost their meaning and produce more anxiety or effort than wonder and delight?

Make some observations, being very honest about what's important to you. For instance, I love planning and preparing special meals, spending time with family and friends, attending candlelight services, and playing and listening to holiday music. I don't always enjoy shopping, wrapping, and decorating. However, your preferences may be the complete opposite. Poll family members or those with whom you spend the holidays to find out what means the most to them. Decide together how you want to celebrate this year.

A few years ago I led an adult spirituality workshop at my church based on the book *Unplug the Christmas Machine*, by Jo Robinson and Jean Staeheli, in which participants and I conducted this type of holiday inventory. We discovered that our holiday spending and gift-giving felt excessive. We found that we (all women in this group) shouldered the bulk of the tasks involved in holiday preparations, often at the price of our self-care and peace of mind. What we all longed for was a simpler, more family-centered and spiritual holiday season. Here are some ideas we shared in a brainstorming session aimed at making this kind of holiday a reality. Perhaps our solutions will help you to reach the same goal:

Simplify gift-giving

Discuss with extended family members and friends ways to simplify gift-giving, for example, by:

- drawing names, giving a family gift, or agreeing not to exchange gifts but to share something special: a meal, performance, or vacation instead of purchasing individual gifts for everyone on your list
- limiting presents to children only
- making presents such as crafts: ornaments, sewn or knitted items, or food: jam, chutney, spiced nuts, bread, cookies, or candy
- setting and sticking to a budget with per-person spending limits (and not buying more for that person if you find bargains)
- giving recycled presents such as flea market or garage sale finds or passing on something of yours
- making a charitable donation in the recipient's name or giving gifts that benefit worthy causes
- giving gift certificates to eliminate returns and exchanges
- giving IOUs for babysitting, baking, (My late father-in-law always relished his "Cookie of the Month" membership.) and personal services

Plan family activities

If family time is a priority for you at this time of year, you may have to turn down invitations to be at home more. To involve the whole family consider:

- working on creative projects such as a gingerbread house, and cinnamon or salt dough ornaments
- baking cookies or breads to bring to neighbors and friends
- decorating a tree for the birds with popcorn and cranberry garlands
- using stamp pads or potato prints to make your own wrapping paper and gift cards
- wrapping and working on cards together
- reading a book together, perhaps John Grisham's *Skipping Christmas* or your favorite holiday stories
- doing puzzles or playing games
- joining in outdoor activities like walking, skating, or sledding

- collaborating on a family mural, photo album, or scrapbook to record the year's shared events

To rekindle the spirit of the season

Look at what contributes to your spiritual experiences or makes you feel most grateful, and weave in more of these activities. These may include:

- listening to, playing, and singing holiday music, inviting friends and family to join in with their voices and instruments
- lighting candles (Almost all traditions celebrate with candles and light: Christian Advent, Jewish Menorah, Kwanzaa's Kinara, and the Pagan Yule log.)
- attending religious services
- being still in meditative or quiet time, even more important during times of hustle and bustle
- taking good care of yourself
- being outdoors and giving yourself time to appreciate the lacy silhouettes of bare tree branches and enjoy the magic of a snowfall, weather permitting
- reconnecting with family and friends via letters cards, phone calls, emails, visits
- reading spiritual texts and holiday stories

However you choose to celebrate, may peace, love, and joy be yours this holiday season and beyond!

Out of Darkness, Light

Here in the Northern Hemisphere, this is the season of darkness. From September 23, the first day of fall and the Autumnal Equinox, the hours of daylight progressively decrease. They will continue to do so until the shortest day and longest night on December 22, which is the Winter Solstice and the first day of winter. The scientific explanation for this is that as the Earth orbits around the sun, it also spins on its axis. It's the gradually changing tilt of the Earth's axis that causes the change in seasons. When we are tilted away from the sun, we receive less direct sunlight and the elevation of the sun is lower. At the Winter Solstice, the Northern Hemisphere is tilted the furthest away from the sun, resulting in the lowest elevation of the sun from the horizon and the shortest number of daylight hours. If the days are feeling dark and dreary, take heart. Things will brighten up after December 22, with a gradual increase in daylight hours. Until then, here are some ways that you can make light of it.

Relish the darkness
Instead of cursing it, you could take advantage of the opportunities darkness offers to:

REST UP—If you find it harder to get out of bed on these dark mornings or find yourself nodding off early in the evening, acknowledge your body's inner cues, and get more sleep. In the natural world, there's a period of cocooning before metamorphosis. Perhaps this mirrors something in your own personal or business life. Give yourself permission to percolate. It may lead to transformation in the New Year.

CELEBRATE THE SEASON—Many of this season's cultural and religious traditions coincide with the Winter Solstice. Many of the rituals and celebrations involve candles, special meals, and gathering with family and friends. All help to lighten our spirits and warm us from the inside out.

TEND TO HEARTH AND HOME—Just as some animals hibernate, this time of year can be the perfect time to hunker down at home. Balance festivities with quiet evenings at home, perhaps by the fire, to experience the holidays as a peaceful, not a frazzled time.

MARVEL AT THE CONTRAST—A dark backdrop makes light appear even more brilliant. Give in to the sense of wonder while stargazing, lighting candles, staring into the flickering flames of a fire, or viewing ornamental light displays.

Bring more light into your life

We can't control the seasons or the weather, but if they begin to affect our mood, we can make some adjustments to bring more light into our lives. Some people, especially those who live in the northern latitudes, suffer from Seasonal Affective Disorder (SAD) during the winter months. Brought on by sunlight deprivation, SAD is characterized by lethargy, carbohydrate cravings, and depression or "the blues" during the winter months. If you are affected by SAD, or if you feel yourself slipping into a funk on overcast or stormy days, here are some steps you can take to bring a little more light into your life:

GET OUTSIDE—I like to break up my work days with a brisk walk outside before or after lunch, when the sun is at its highest point and it feels the warmest.

USE FULL SPECTRUM LIGHTING—In her December, 2002 issue of *Health Wisdom for Women*, Christiane Northrup, M.D heartily recommends using light boxes, full-spectrum desk lamps, and/or full-spectrum light bulbs to create health. In her article, "Brighten up Winter with the Right Kind of Light" she describes studies which indicate that full spectrum lighting can improve mood-boosting serotonin levels, physical fitness, calcium absorption, cancer prevention, school performance, and Vitamin D levels, which help prevent cancer.

BASK IN THE SUN—Sunroofs, skylights, and southern-facing windows can all provide good sources of natural light. Take advantage of sunny days by opening the blinds and taking a sunbath.

HEAD SOUTH—If you are planning a mid-winter vacation, choose a sunny destination. If travel's not in your budget, then consider armchair travel. Read a book that takes place in the summer, such as Barbara Kingsolver's *Prodigal Summer*, or in a warm setting, such as *Cane River* by Lalita Tademy, or transports you to a desired setting, as *Under the Tuscan Sun* by Frances Mayes will. For those who would like a more tangible experience of the exotic, *Weekends Away (Without Leaving Home): The Ultimate*

World Party Theme Book, published by Conari Press, offers many great ideas for experiencing a weekend get-away without the expense or inconvenience of travel.

May you find the perfect balance between light and dark during this holiday season.

~~~~~~~~~~~~~~~~~~~~~~~~~~~~~~~~~~~~~~~

Resources:

Serving Fire: Food for Thought, Body, and Soul, by Anne Scott

www.religioustolerance.org/winter_solstice.htm—Visit this site to learn more about the solstice and the different ways it's celebrated.

Health Wisdom for Women, by Christiane Northrup, M.D
~~~~~~~~~~~~~~~~~~~~~~~~~~~~~~~~~~~~~~~

A Dream of Connection

I believe that we are all connected. I think our actions and thoughts have a ripple effect and can impact, not only those close by, but also others far away. An uncanny personal experience confirmed this mysterious connection for me.

The morning of December 23, 2004, I woke up remembering a vivid, upsetting dream. In my dream, my husband and I were scuba diving in a tropical ocean when suddenly we were caught up in a tidal wave. It was terrifying. We held hands tightly so as not to lose each other as we let the wave take us. There was no way to fight against its power. We survived, with injuries, but learned that thousands of others did not.

I often have dreams that are relevant to my daily life. At first I thought this was another one of those. Indeed, that day turned out to a stormy one for us, as the holidays, perhaps more accurately described as "Hi-Low-Days," worked to intensify emotions in our household. My normally even-keeled husband sank lower than I'd ever seen, weighed down with sadness over his father's death earlier in the year and frustration over a couple of business deals that fell apart. Although I did my best to support him and stay positive, by that evening, I felt my spirits sinking. As in my dream, we stuck together and pulled through, going on to celebrate a wonderful, relaxing Christmas and New Year's.

Our troubles certainly paled in comparison when, a few days later, I learned of a terrible tsunami in the Indian Ocean and the staggering death tolls left in its wake. The hair on the back of my neck stood up when I first heard about it because it was eerily similar to my recent dream. I had never had that type of prophetic dream before. Since then I've learned that it's quite common for people to have dreams and visions before natural disasters. The experience strongly reinforced my belief that we are all connected.

As we experienced in the aftermath of September 11, the world united after this tragedy as well. There was a tremendous outpouring of sympathy and support for those devastated by the disaster. People dug deep into their pockets to donate to relief organizations. Others literally lent a helping hand, such as one NH doctor spotlighted in our local news who volunteered her time overseas. Many more banded together in spirit, sending prayers of hope to those in affected countries. Wouldn't it be wonderful if it didn't take a tragic event of this magnitude to elicit this response?

I think it is in our human nature to help others. On some level we all feel a connection to each other. What can you do to honor and support this connection? The New Year is a time to reflect upon the past and plan for the future. As you set your intentions for the coming year, look for ways to enhance both your life and the lives of others.

If there's anything positive we can learn in the wake of disasters, perhaps it is that life and connection are precious gifts to cherish and acknowledge because we never know when they might be swept away.

May Peace Prevail

One December morning, as I sat by our picture window looking out over falling snow, I felt as if the world had issued me an invitation to peace, which I accepted. I plugged in the lights of the Christmas tree and saw the lights reflected in the window panes. They appeared as tiny bright spots shining in the blur of the swirling snow. I was surprised to see the snow stick to the ground because the ground was far from frozen with the mild weather we'd been having. (We'd had many days in the 50's, which is unusual for New England in December.) As I sat in stillness and watched, the snow began to frost trees and cover the ground with a blanket of white. I love the muffled sound of snow. Unlike the pitter-pattering or pelting of rain, to my ears, snow makes the sound of hush.

It's easy this time of year to get caught up in the whirl of holiday festivities and miss opportunities for stillness and peace. The list is long, but it can wait. I embraced the moment the morning offered, took some deep breaths, closed my eyes, and felt a warm sensation as the feeling of peace spread outward from my heart to envelop me. I knew then that I could walk in peace the entire day, this whole season, and for my entire life.

Sadly, however, there's ongoing strife in the world. We still have troops in Iraq, atrocities continue in Darfur, and almost every week there's a report of a suicide bombing in some part of the world. Clearly, peace hasn't spread to every corner of the world—yet.

Rather than throw our hands up in hopelessness and helplessness, the first step is to find peace within our own hearts. The way to peace may come in many forms. It could be:

- answering the beckoning call to step away from busyness and enter stillness
- creating a timeless tradition or ritual that soothes the soul
- settling into a quiet acceptance that the holiday season holds both darkness and light
- honoring a desire to give up a struggle and finally forgive (ourselves or others)

However it comes to you, one of the best presents you could

receive this holiday season is the presence of peace.

- How does peace find its way to you?
- How do you let it take root and grow?

Once we discover and step into peace ourselves, we can then bring it out into the world. Slowly it will spread. Some religious traditions have a lovely ritual of "passing the peace." People shake hands and greet each other with the words "Peace be with you."

- How can you pass the peace?

As we end one year and move into the next, I'd like to close with the words I remember the minister of my hometown church always used as a benediction: "May the peace that passes all understanding be and abide with you now and forevermore."

Full Circle

Congratulations! You've now come full circle, reaching the end of another year and the end of this book. Is this an ending, however, or is it a beginning?

Growth follows a spiraling path. Throughout the course of your life, you will often return to the same places. You approach each round from a new level of perspective. With each pass you create different experiences. For this reason I encourage you to dip back into this book in the coming months and years. As you continue to evolve, may this book guide you to greater joy and balance.

Before you turn the page of your calendar or the lens of your kaleidoscope of life, please take time to pause and reflect upon the past year and celebrate the steps you've taken.

- What were the highlights of the year and what made them so special?
- What were your greatest accomplishments?
- What did you not accomplish that you'd hoped to?
- Who have you become?
- How have you made a difference?
- Who and what have you treasured the most?
- Are you pleased with the direction your life is taking? Why or why not?
- What lessons have you learned?
- What's next?

And so the journey continues.

Acknowledgments

It takes a village to raise a child. It's taken at least that to support this first-time author. First and foremost, I want to thank my mother, Frances Honich, who has always been my biggest cheerleader and my best editor.

I'm grateful for the expertise and professionalism of my editor, Susannah Abbott, my graphic designer, Mary Chiodo, my photographer, Mike Lutch, of www.waggingtailsphotography. I'm indebted to my eagle eye proofreaders: Bette Durfee, Laurie Geary, Lorri-Ann Charron, Judy Perkins, and Sue Solomon who helped me polish my manuscript.

I deeply appreciate the great coaching I've had over the years from Alan Seale, Soleira Green, Zoran Todorovich, Jane McAllister Dukes, Ushma Patel, Margaret Krigbaum, and Judy Irving, which has been instrumental in my ongoing evolution.

I value the roles that Bob Crutchfield, Lee Bluemel, Gail Forseyth-Vail, Frank Clarkson, all the folks at The North Parish, the goddesses in my Cakes groups, Susan Richards, Brian Tronic, and my other yoga instructors have played in my spiritual development.

I'm grateful for all my teachers and mentors over the years: C. J. Hayden, Laura Berman Fortgang, Cheryl Richardson, Pamela Richarde, Patricia Holman, the late Thomas J. Leonard, Dave Buck, Sam Horn, and the faculty (now colleagues) at Coach Inc.

I've lost count of the times I've been uplifted or inspired by members of my coaching community, especially Vicki Ball, Kate Carleton, Ginny O'Brien, Chrissy Carrew, Lydia Roy, Kerul Kassel, Dorothy Eckes, Lynn Cohen, Susan Abrams, Deborah Roth, Cassi Christensen, Jeanne McLellan, Ann Marie Leary, Donna Steinhorn, and my fellow ICFNE and ICF-NE Board members.

The emails and encouragement from my monthly newsletter subscribers and clients have kept me writing and growing.

My deepest thanks goes to the members of my immediate family—Bill, Sam, and Alex—and extended family who have provided the inspiration for much of my material. Thanks for your unconditional love and support.

Bibliography

Breathnach, Sarah Ban. *Simple Abundance: A Daybook of Comfort and Joy.* New York: Warner Books, 1995.

Byrne, Rhonda. *The Secret.* New York: Atria Books/Beyond Words, 2006.

Covey, Stephen. *The 7 Habits of Highly Effective People: Powerful Lessons in Personal Change.* New York: Fireside/ Simon and Schuster, 1989.

Cameron, Julia. *The Artist's Way: A Spiritual Path to Higher Creativity.* New York: J.P. Tartcher/Putnam Publishing Group, 1992.

Chopra, M.D., Deepak. *Ageless Body, Timeless Mind.* New York: Harmony Books/Crown Publishing, 1993.

CoachInc.com. *The Coach U Personal Development Workbook and Guide.* Hoboken, NJ: John Wiley & Sons, 2005.

CoachInc.com. *The Coach U Personal and Corporate Coach Training Handbook.* Hoboken, New Jersey: John Wiley & Sons, 2005.

Grabhorn, Lynn. *Excuse Me Your Life is Waiting: The Astonishing Power of Feelings,* Charlottesville, VA: Hampton Rhodes Publishing Company, 2000.

http://www.holidayorigins.com

Dalai Lama and Howard C. Culter. *The Art of Happiness: A Handbook for Living*. New York: Riverhead Books, Penguin Putnam Inc., 1998.

"Exercise and Aging: Can You Walk Away from Father Time?" *Harvard Men's Health Watch,* December 2005. Retrieved from http://www.health.harvard.edu/newsletters/Harvard_Mens_Health_Watch.htm

Hill, Napoleon. Think and Grow Rich. New York: Random House, 1960.

Hock, Dee W. and Visa International. *Birth of the Chaordic Age.* San Francisco: Berrett-Koehler Publishers, 2000.

http:www.motivational-inspirational-corner.com

Northrup, M.D., Christiane. *Women's Bodies, Women's Wisdom.* New York: Bantam Books, 1998.

Northrup, M.D., Christiane. "Brighten up Winter with the Right Kind of Light" *Health Wisdom for Women*, December, 2002.

Pink, Daniel. *A Whole New Mind: Why Right-Brainers Will Rule the Future.* New York: Riverhead Trade, 2006.

http://quotations.about.com/cs/inspirationquotes

http:www.quoteland.com

Ray, Rebecca and John Schmitt. *No-Vacation Nation* Center for Economic and Policy Research, May 2007. Retrieved from www.cepr.net/documents/publications/working_time_2007_05.pdf

Ribokas, Bob. "The Geology of the Grand Canyon," http://www.bobspixels.com/kaibab.org/geology/gc_geol.htm

Richardson, Cheryl. *Stand Up for Your Life: A Practical Step-by-Step Plan to Build Inner Confidence and Personal Power.*

Robinson, Jo and Jean Staeheli. *Unplug the Christmas Machine*. New York: Harper Paperbacks, 1991.

Robinson, Lynn. *Divine Intuition: Your Guide to Creating a Life You Love*. New York: Dorling Kindersley, 2001.

Rowling, J. K. *Harry Potter and the Prisoner of Azkaban.* New York: Scholastic Press, 1999.

Rao, Joe. *Mars Watch: Complete Viewing Guide.* Special to www.Space.com

Seale, Alan. *Soul Mission, Life Vision: Recognize Your True Gifts and Make Your Mark Upon the World.* Boston: Red Wheel, 2003.

http://scienceworld.wolfram.com/astronomy/WinterSolstice.html

Twist, Lynne. *The Soul of Money: Transforming Your Relationship with Money and Life*. New York: W. W. Norton & Company, 2003.

Webster's College Dictionary. New York: Random House, 1991

Whitworth, Laura, Henry Kimsey-House, and Phil Sandahl, *Co-active Coaching: New Skills for Coaching People Toward Success in Work and Life.* Palo Alto: Davies-Black Publishing, 1998.

http://www.workingmother.com

Zander, Rosumund Stone and Benjamin Zander. *The Art of Possibility*. New York: Penguin Books, 2002.

Topical Index

Endnotes

[1] National Center for Health Statistics, *The Propensity of Overweight and Obesity Among Adults: United States 2003-2004,* retrieved July 20, 2007 from, http://www.cdc.gov/nchs/products/pubs/pubd/hestats/overweight/overwght_adult_03.htm

[2] World Health Organization, *Chronic Diseases: Major Cause of Death*, retrieved July 20, 2007 from, http://www.who.int/chp/chronic_disease_report/part1/en/index1.html

[3] Isaacs, Nora. "Sweet Slumber," *Yoga Journal*, August 2007. *Sweet Slumber*, by Nora Isaacs Yoga Journal, August 2007

[4] http://David Usborne, *Filmmaker Records Effects of Only Eating at McDonald's for a Month*, January 25, 2004, retrieved July 20, 2007 from, http://www.geocities.com/missionstmichael/FastFood.html

[5] Retrieved April 4, 2006 from, http://www.thomasedison.com http://www.thomasedison.com

[6] "Exercise and aging: Can you walk away from Father Time?" *Harvard Men's Health Watch,* December 2005, retrieved July 20, 2007 from, http://www.health.harvard.edu/newsletters/Harvard_Mens_Health_Watch.htm

[7] Retrieved September 3, 2006 from, http://www.timeday.org http://www.timeday.org

[8] Bellis, Mary, *The Invention of VELCRO, George de Mestral*, retrieved July 20, 2007 from, http://inventors.about.com/library/weekly/11091207.htm

[9] Retrieved August 15, 2007 from, http://www.casafamilyday.org

To support you in your journey, visit www.balancewithgrace.com or call (978)689-7446 or (888)833-1903 to learn more about Grace's:

- individual, group, co-op, and mentor coaching
- keynotes
- workshops
- retreats
- audio programs
- free monthly email newsletter
- blog